KU-416-540

KEY FACTS

HUMAN RIGHTS

PETER HALSTEAD

Hodder Arnold

A MEMBER OF THE HODDER HEADLINE GROUP

Orders: please contact Bookpoint Ltd, 130 Milton Park, Abingdon, Oxon OX14 4SB.
Telephone: (44) 01235 827720. Fax: (44) 01235 400454. Lines are open from 9.00–6.00,
Monday to Saturday, with a 24-hour message answering service.
You can also order through our website: hoddereducation.co.uk

British Library Cataloguing in Publication Data
A catalogue record for this title is available from The British Library.

ISBN-10: 0 340 88696 X
ISBN-13: 978 0 340 88696 0

First published 2005
Impression number   10 9 8 7 6 5 4 3 2 1
Year   2010 2009 2008 2007 2006 2005

Copyright © 2005 Peter Halstead

Hodder Headline's policy is to use papers that are natural, renewable and recyclable products
and made from wood grown in sustainable forests. The logging and manufacturing processes
are expected to conform to the environmental regulations of the country of origin.

Typeset by Transet Limited, Coventry, England.
Printed in Great Britain for Hodder Arnold, an imprint of Hodder Education, a member of the
Hodder Headline Group, 338 Euston Road, London NW1 3BH by Cox & Wyman Ltd,
Reading, Berks.

CONTENTS

PREFACE

The Key Facts series is designed to give a clear view of each subject. This will be useful to students when tackling new topics and is invaluable as a revision aid. Most chapters open with an outline in diagram form of the points covered in that chapter. The points are then developed in list form to make learning easier. Supporting cases are given throughout by name and for some complex areas the facts of cases are given to reinforce the point being made.

The Key Facts series is a practical and complete revision aid that can be used by students of law courses at all levels from A level to degree and beyond, and in professional and vocational courses. Largely as a result of the Human Rights Act 1998, this subject is now widely studied not only by students of law but by people interested in many other disciplines. This book deals with human rights in the UK and Europe, but its scope is considerably wider in that it addresses other regional regimes and global human rights, with chapters on underlying theory, rights and remedies, and a variety of specific themes.

Anyone who needs to study the subject for academic purposes, or who is interested in human rights and wants a comprehensive source or revision book, should find this book particulary helpful.

The law is stated as I believe it to be on 1st January 2005.

CHAPTER 1

INTRODUCTION TO HUMAN RIGHTS

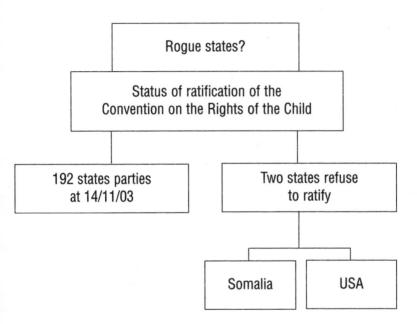

1.1 OVERVIEW

1. There has been considerable interest in human rights in the UK in recent years since the Labour Party, then in opposition, promised to 'bring rights home' at the 1997 General Election by incorporating the bulk of the European Convention on Human Rights into domestic law, eventually implemented by the Human Rights Act 1998.

2. This encouraged schools, colleges and universities to give high priority to providing courses on human rights, although much of the emphasis has been on changes in UK law, and to a lesser extent on European developments.

3. Although the European regional human rights regime is advanced and successful, it only constitutes a fraction of the totality of human rights.

4. This book takes a broader view so that students are introduced to the background and theory of rights, as well as the global system and regional regimes, thematic concerns, rights and remedies, while not neglecting the growth of human rights in Europe and the UK.

5. Using this book both as an introductory guide and revision aid, students will obtain a broad understanding of the main aspects of local, regional and global human rights.

1.2 HUMAN RIGHTS LANGUAGE

References to particular organisations and treaties should be clear from the context, but knowledge of the following commonly used contractions will be useful:

CEDAW	The Convention on the Elimination of all forms of Discrimination against Women
ECHR	May mean European Convention, Commission or Court of Human Rights, depending on the context
ECOSOC	(UN) Economic and Social Council
ICC	International Criminal Court
ICCPR	International Covenant on Civil and Political Rights
ICESCR	International Covenant on Economic, Social and Cultural Rights
ICJ	International Court of Justice
ICRC	International Committee of the Red Cross
ILO	International Labour Organisation
INGO	International Non Governmental Organisation
NGO	Non Governmental Organisation
UDHR	Universal Declaration of Human Rights
UN	United Nations
UNHCHR	United Nations High Commissioner for Human Rights
UNHCR	United Nations High Commissioner for Refugees

1.2.2 Glossary

Civil and political rights: first generation citizens' rights to liberty and equality.

Collective rights: the rights of native aboriginal groups to have their rights as a whole protected, as opposed to individual rights such as to a fair hearing.

Convention: a legally binding agreement between states, entered into voluntarily and enforceable only to the extent acknowledged by signatories, and used more or less interchangeably with the words **covenant** and **treaty**.

Covenant: see **Convention**.

Customary international law: in domestic terms, roughly the equivalent to common law, as opposed to treaties, which can be compared to statutes.

Declaration: a set of non-legally binding standards to be observed by states.

Economic, social and cultural rights: second generation rights giving people rights to the material necessities of life, rather than to individual freedoms.

Environmental and development rights: third generation rights of mankind to have a safe and healthy environment, and for peoples generally to live in harmony.

International Bill of Human Rights: the combined totality of the UDHR, ICESCR, ICCPR and its optional protocol.

Protocol: an addendum to a treaty which modifies it, often used to incorporate optional provisions not acceptable to all states parties.

Ratification: confirmation by a state's legislative machinery of adherence to a convention.

State: a territorial area occupied by a society that possesses the same government and accepts the same laws; states are mostly synonymous with countries.

Treaty: see **Convention**.

CHAPTER 2

HUMAN RIGHTS THEORY

Rights may be:
- civil
- political
- economic
- social
- cultural
- generational

Concepts of rights may be:
- universal
- inalienable
- interconnected
- interrelated
- indivisible
- obligational, ie including responsibilities

HUMAN RIGHTS THEORY

Natural and human rights theorists include:
- Thomas Hobbes
- John Locke
- Rousseau
- Immanuel Kant
- Wesley Hohfeld
- Lon Fuller
- John Rawls
- John Finnis
- Jack Donnelly

Rights may be comparative or contrasting:
- universal/relative
- collective/individual
- positive/negative
- active/passive
- right/rights
- moral/legal
- natural justice/legal justice
- claim rights/liberty rights
- will theory/interest theory

2.1 APPROACHES TO HUMAN RIGHTS THEORY

2.1.1 The 'UN' approach

1. There are many ways of theorising about or categorising human rights, the more usual being:
- civil;
- political;
- economic;
- social;
- cultural.

2. Modern human rights are built primarily on Western notions of individually based civil and political rights.

3. The Cold War (1945–89) brought out a conflicting approach from the Soviet bloc, which preferred to emphasise economic and social rights.

4. The emergence of the Third World from colonial subservience after the Second World War led to advocacy for cultural and developmental rights.

5. There are analogies here to Karel Vasak's generational theory, discussed below.

2.1.2 A conceptual approach

1. Another method is to describe human rights as being:
- universal;
- inalienable;
- interconnected;
- interrelated;
- indivisible;
- obligational, ie including responsibilities.

2. The problem with using such descriptions is that they are sweeping, sometimes tautologous, and tend to ignore the practicalities of how human rights actually operate in the modern world: eg not explaining what is meant by interconnected or indivisible.

2.1.3 A comparative or contrasting analysis

1. Often comparative or contrasting approaches are used, some of which overlap in meaning, including:
   * universal/relative;
   * collective/individual;
   * positive/negative;
   * active/passive;
   * right/rights;
   * moral/legal;
   * natural justice/legal justice;
   * claim rights/liberty rights;
   * will theory/interest theory.
2. This is a popular, albeit simplistic, way of explaining the ideas behind human rights, because it focuses attention on specific but limited aspects of their nature.

2.1.4 Writers and practitioners of natural and human rights

1. Another common methodological approach is to consider individual writers, or to trace a line of philosophers who have contributed to the growth of particular strands of natural and human rights theory.
2. Such earlier European philosophers would include:
   * Thomas Hobbes (1588–1679);
   * John Locke (1632–1704);
   * Jean Jacques Rousseau (1712–78);
   * Immanuel Kant (1724–1804);
3. Twentieth-century and contemporary writers on human rights would include:
   * Wesley Hohfeld (1879–1918);
   * John Rawls (1921–2002);
   * John Finnis (1940–);
   * Jack Donnelly (1951–).

4. This chapter is about theory, but human rights are also often measured by the great 'practitioners', whose writings or political achievements were also influential, eg:
   * Mohandas Karamchand (Mahatma) Ghandi (1869–1948);
   * Eleanor Roosevelt (1884–1962);
   * Nwlaon Eoliklalla (Nelson) Mandela (1918–);
   * Aung San Suu Kyi (1946 –).

2.2 THE 'UN' APPROACH

2.2.1 Why 'UN' approach?

1. Labelling civil, political, economic, social and cultural rights as the 'UN' approach is:
   a) shorthand to summarise the main thrust of the way that mid- and late-eighteenth century rights theory developed into twentieth and twenty-first century international and regional rights regimes;
   b) 'regimes' means quasi-legal systems with limited enforcement mechanisms that are frequently overlooked or ignored for political and economic reasons.
2. The forces that drove the early movements towards human rights had some of their origins in seventeenth century English events, but were primarily fuelled by the American and French revolutions in the late eighteenth century.
3. Karel Vasak's generational theory reflected this; propounded in 1979, it provided a metaphorical explanation of how rights came to be formulated and suggested how they might be recognised as continuing to be developed.

2.2.2 Karel Vasak's third generation rights

1. Vasak's generational theory suggests the development of human rights is (metaphorically) equivalent to the French

revolutionary slogan *liberté, equalité and fraternité*, giving us first, second and third generations of human rights development.

2. *Liberté* provides first generation rights, which:
   ● are civil and political in nature;
   ● are designed to protect citizens from excesses perpetrated by the state;
   ● are fundamentally negative in nature eg aticles 3–21 of the Universal Declaration and the ICCPR;
   ● in practice, comprise freedoms such as religion, speech, fair trial, etc.

3. *Egalité* characterises second generational rights, based on social, economic and cultural factors. They are mostly positive and would:
   ● include employment and family rights as contained in articles 22–7 of the Universal Declaration and the ICESC;
   ● require states to institute programmes that would benefit the individual.

4. *Fraternité* means solidarity, implying group and collective rights such as those of peoples to self-determination and their own economic, social and cultural development, much less evident in the conventional global human rights regime.

5. Specifically these would relate to rights to:
   ● development;
   ● peace;
   ● a healthy environment;
   ● ownership of the common heritage of mankind (eg the seabed);
   ● communication.

6. This moves beyond consideration of the individual *per se* and extends human rights to community and interactive areas and issues, reflecting globalisation trends.

7. The essential characteristics of third generation rights are the imposition of:
   ● joint obligations on all states;
   ● further obligations wider than those on States, extending

to international actors such as INGOs and transnational corporations;

- obligations on peoples as a whole, rather than on individuals.

8. Vasak's theory helps to explain the process of 'concretisation' of rights from theoretical idealism prior to the American and French revolutions, to practical implementation after the Second World War.

9. An example would be the 1986 UN Declaration on the Right to Development, together with various documents, charters and treaties providing support for the emergence of fraternal rights to peace and a healthy environment.

10. The use of the generational metaphor is not meant to imply the demise of previous generations and their subsequent replacement.

11. There is debate about whether solidarity implies:
   a) a quantitative or qualitative shift in the nature of human rights;
   b) the birth of entirely new rights, or extensions of the old, ie are the joint responsibilities of developmental rights of a different nature to previously recognised individual rights?

12. Opposition to Vasak's theory has been based on differing suppositions:
   - human rights are individual and enforceable by law, but solidarity rights are collective and not capable of legal enforcement;
   - that attempting to add these to the rights currently accepted in the International Bill of Human Rights will dilute the efficacy of those fundamental rights and freedoms.

13. Vasak's theory is an elegant theoretical approach to understanding the origins, development, implementation and possible future trends of international human rights, but not meant to be interpreted as a literal application of the French revolutionary slogan.

2.3 A CONCEPTUAL APPROACH

1. The use of the word 'inalienable' is usually taken to mean that human rights cannot be:
   - bought and sold;
   - inherited;
   - given away;
   - otherwise disposed of:
   a) by the person who holds the right in question;
   b) by that person on someone else's behalf (eg his or her child).

2. For example, a person does not possess the power to sell or give him or herself into slavery, servitude or forced labour, even voluntarily.

3. Interconnected, interrelated and indivisible rights apply to all human beings by virtue of their very humanity, and mean that the various rights and freedoms contained or referred to in many documents and treaties are:
   - interdependent;
   - not to be ranked in order of perceived importance;
   - not to be qualified or reduced any further than is clearly provided for in particular instruments (many rights being qualified rather than absolute, as can be seen in the European Convention on Human Rights).

4. 'Obligational' means that rights are connected to correlative responsibilities and are not simply free-standing claims that individuals or peoples can call upon in a vacuum; eg Hohfeld's analysis.

5. 'Universal' is also a commonly used word, the contrast here usually being with (cultural) relativity, dealt with in the next section.

2.4 A CONTRASTING OR COMPARATIVE ANALYSIS

2.4.1 Universal or relative human rights?

1. The universal theory of human rights posits the idea that there is an international paradigm that must be applied uniformly across the world.
2. This is the theory behind the United Nations' Universal Declaration and the twin international covenants that together make up the International Bill of Human Rights.
3. Cultural relativism is the counter-argument that human rights, some of which may be desirable but not essential, are not uniform or necessarily based on individual civil and political rights, but vary across the world according to:
    - differing cultural practices;
    - the reality of huge variations in economic and social development in different continents, countries and societies.
4. A significant weakness of the cultural relativity approach is that it is often used by ruling politicians or elites in states where the population are unable freely to express their views.
5. An important weakness of the universal argument is that although it proclaims itself to be God-given and self-evident, the fact remains that human rights are not universally respected, observed or applied.

2.4.2 Collective or individual rights?

1. The English, American and French traditions particularly influenced the modern world system, which tends towards the universal and individual, reflecting a mature democratic background and considerable personal material security.
2. Others, coming from different and less affluent cultures, argue that collective rights which aim to protect groups of people or complete societies are more important, as for example the need to protect:

- *children* in the global context more than an individual's right to (say) freedom of speech;
- *workers* who may be exploited by powerful transnationals to produce goods for lucrative markets and affluent consumers;
- *subsistence dwellers* whose need for the basics of life – clean water, food, health care and education – appear more cogent than freedom of thought or belief.

2.4.3 Positive or negative rights?

1. Positive human rights are not universally acknowledged. They arise from Rousseau's continental tradition under which the state should provide equality, education, health care and the means of earning a living and supporting the family; alternatively these are sometimes referred to as welfare rights.
2. The negative approach stems more from the English and American tradition, which tends to believe that rights comprise things that government should not be allowed to do to the individual; documents illustrating this include Magna Carta, and the English and American Bills of Rights.
3. Examples of both positive and negative approaches are found in modern global and regional regimes.
4. An alternative way of classifying *negative* rights is as active or passive:
   - 'active' implies ability to do what one chooses;
   - 'passive' comprise rights to be exercised at will.

2.4.4 Right or rights?

1. Originally what are now recognised as human rights (however defined) were called natural rights, and arose out of man's need to try to explain his place in the universe.
2. Later natural law theory became more refined and sophisticated, and tended to be founded on a monotheistic view of life, but still only implying relatively few principles.

3. The modern approach changed the emphasis from natural to human rights, and started to provide long lists of individual rights possessed by or attributed to human beings, eg specialist treaties relating to children, women, slavery, genocide etc.

2.4.5 Moral or legal rights?

1. In theory the distinction is simple:
   a) legal rights exist in legal systems, enforceable within states and between states, but only where they are bound by treaty or under legitimate international compulsion;
   b) moral 'rights' are better described as moral claims, as they are not legally enforceable under either system.
2. If rights are accepted as being objective, of high priority and universal, it is implicit that compliance with them is mandatory and the conclusion can be drawn that they are moral in origin.
3. However, if they are subjective and culturally relative, then universal compliance will not apply and observance of them would depend on legal rules within particular jurisdictions.
4. In practice, human rights are made to apply (albeit patchily) in both the moral and legal spheres, although mostly imposed by legal machinery.
5. Moral imperatives drive the search for justice following such international crimes as ethnic cleansing or genocide, evidenced by the Rwanda and former Yugoslavia tribunals.

2.4.6 Natural justice or legal justice?

1. The origins of human rights can be found approximately 2,500 years ago in Greek philosophy through notions of natural law and justice, connected but not identical ideas.
2. Natural justice could be found in innate conscience-driven ideas of fairness, rightness and wrongness; it is subjective and differs from one person, society and generation to the next.

3. Legal justice stems from legal rules imposed by particular states or leaders of societies on those within their power and jurisdiction, and stems from legal positivism, ie the laws and rules that are imposed (posited) by those holding or granted power to rule over others.

4. In England these ideas were developed in the nineteenth century by Jeremy Bentham, John Austin and John Stuart Mill, and in the twentieth century the concept of justice as fairness was promulgated by John Rawls.

5. Legal positivism did not have much to say about human rights as now understood, although Mill's ideas on utilitarianism suggested that the greatest good of the greatest number would contribute towards human happiness, albeit at a price.

2.4.7 Claim rights and liberty rights

1. These originate in Wesley Hohfeld's theory published in 1919, attempting a thorough classification of what he identified as four differing types of right:
   - liberty rights;
   - claim rights;
   - power rights;
   - immunity rights.

2. In recent years there has been a tendency to integrate these into two composite types:
   - liberty rights;
   - claim rights.

3. Claim rights are thought to be of primary importance and are defined as rights that are owed a duty, to which there may be positive or negative claims:
   a) a positive claim right applies to a particular thing (ie a good or service) which someone else has a positive duty to provide;
   b) a negative claim right is one with which you have to prevent someone else interfering, eg by threatening your health or wellbeing.

4. A further sub-division is that claim rights can be held either against a person (*in personam*) or a thing (*in rem*).

5. Liberty rights are things you can do which are not prohibited, so they are mainly negative; eg no one can stop you from exercising your liberty right to dine at the Ritz.

6. The corollary is that no one has a positive duty to make it possible for you to be able to afford to do so; thus liberty rights provide the ability to be free to do something without willing the necessary means.

2.4.8 Will theory or interests theory?

1. This involves the question of whether human rights are self-evident, or need justification.

2. If they are self-evident they would arise from an empirical set of facts perceivable in the world, from which arise duties and obligations that humans recognise and observe.

3. However, the validity of human rights in the real world requires them to be made choate by means of legal machinery, which is itself based upon tangible and justifiable principles.

4. Interests theorists believe that the main purpose of human rights is to further basic human interests and needs, identifying the things that humans need to live purposeful lives in a state of wellbeing.

5. This viewpoint is represented by John Rawls who identifies the basic forms of human goods as being:
- life and its capacity for development;
- acquisition of knowledge, as an end in itself;
- capacity for recreation;
- aesthetic expression;
- sociability and friendship;
- practical reasonableness;
- capacity for intelligent and reasonable thought processes;
- religion, or the capacity for spiritual experience.

6. Earlier philosophers such as Thomas Hobbes put forward their own practical reasons why interests should form a foundation for human rights.

7. Cultural relativists criticise this approach, as the basic forms of human goods are not universal and what would pass in, say, the Sudan or Myanma (Burma) would be unacceptable to an American or European.

8. Will theory argues that the validity of human rights in philosophical terms is based on the human need and capacity for freedom.

9. Hart took the view that all men had an equal right to be free, and that all the things people wanted to do could be achieved if they had the one thing necessary, ie freedom to exercise their will.

10. Others, such as Ronald Dworkin, Henry Shue and Alan Gewirth have developed versions of will theory that in different ways base human rights on the idea of personal autonomy.

11. One problem facing this approach is that not all humans have (sufficient) autonomy (eg children and people with mental or physical incapacity), so if will theory is right, how could they claim human rights when they are unable to exercise the will that would bring them into play?

2.5 GENERAL DEVELOPMENT OF RIGHTS

1. The expression 'human rights' came into general use after 1945, although probably first used by Henry Thoreau in the previous century, and at their simplest they can be defined as rights belonging to individuals by virtue of the fact that they are human.

2. Rights can be traced in Western philosophy to Stoic natural law doctrines, ideas that originated with Zeno of Citium, the Stoics teaching that there were pervasive laws of nature and man's conduct should therefore be measured in accordance with those laws.

3. Roman law developed the idea of natural law into a law of nations, whose universal provenance fitted in neatly with

their conquest of the then known world and their desire to foster colonisation and trade.

4. In the Dark and Middle Ages the Catholic Church through theologians such as St Augustine and Thomas Aquinas developed these ideas for its own purposes, distinguishing man-made laws and those of God, but 'rights' still had a very different meaning from that of modern times recognising, for example, the legitimacy of holy wars and slavery.

5. With the Renaissance and Treaty of Westphalia (1648) began the modern notion of sacrosanct states in which various populations worked out their relationships to their rulers.

6. Later in the Age of the Enlightenment, the growth of knowledge encouraged a more rational and scientific approach to rights, with people starting to base their beliefs on empirical methodology and observation rather than solely on nature or God.

7. Revolutions in Europe and the Americas brought practical expression and effect to the development of rights, albeit with resistance from those who believed that rights should depend on laws made by rulers and not on rhetorical nonsense on stilts, as Jeremy Bentham called them.

8. Dreadful experiences in the first half of the twentieth century put paid to most general ideas that rights came from God:

   - Marxism taught that rights could only be claimed by revolution.
   - Liberalism taught that rights had to be turned into universal norms and where practicable made enforceable.
   - The Cold War demonstrated that power blocs will cynically use different versions of rights to further their own political and economic interests.
   - States emerging from colonialism refused automatically to accept pre-conceived versions, Western or modified, preferring their own cultural versions.

9. In the early twenty-first century, in the post-Cold War era, the next stage of development of human rights is taking place, with general acceptance that some human rights are universal, although:
- agreement by some states is grudging and half-hearted;
- there are very few states where human rights are always placed first and foremost and which never allow political and economic means to justify the end;
- there is equivocal and restricted agreement as to which rights should be accorded universality.

10. An example of this is the UN Convention on the Rights of the Child, perhaps the most widely accepted human rights convention with 192 states acceding to the treaty, and only the US and Somalia recalcitrant.

11. Despite that fact, there is worldwide mistreatment of children including:
- slave labour and enforced servitude;
- child soldiers;
- failure to provide basic health care and elementary education;
- ethnic cleansing;
- child prostitution.

12. So the fact that governments nominally accept the modern universal norm, and cannot allow themselves to be seen denying its tenets and implications, does not mean that they agree to establish a really effective enforceable global regime or to be bound by aspects of it that do not suit their purposes.

13. The rationale behind this reluctant acceptance of human rights remains vague and diverse, with different states at different times relying on ideas that include the:
- divine;
- ethical;
- moral;
- legal;
- culturally relative;

- socially contractarian;
- redistributive;
- utilitarian.

14. These, and other approaches, can be linked to the varying theories of rights discussed in this chapter and although there have been encouraging post-Cold War developments, these are counter-balanced and sometimes negated by the increasing uncertainties facing the world in the twenty-first century.

CHAPTER 3
THE GLOBAL REGIME

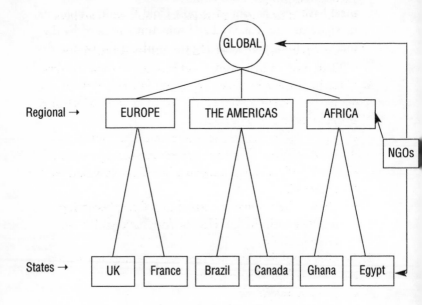

3.1 UN CHARTER AND DECLARATION

3.1.1 Principles, ideals and motivations

1. The global human rights regime established after the Second World War had a number of underlying principles, ideals and motivations, including the need for:
   - an urgent response to the recent horrors and atrocities;
   - a framework broadly based on civil and political ideas of what human rights should be, derived mainly from English, American and French history and sources;
   - strengthening international criminal law.

2. This chapter deals with global human rights in the context of international law, although many breaches of human rights occur within individual states.

3. Ideas for an effective global system of human rights were circulated during the war because:
- the failed League of Nations had omitted to address them;
- the emerging extent of Nazi atrocities required the definition of new crimes and machinery to tackle them.

4. It was impossible to obtain complete agreement on all matters that might have been included in an ideal scheme, as the following timelines show:
- 1945 – UN Charter established the 'club rules';
- 1948 – UDHR expressed unenforceable aspirations;
- 1966 – ICCPR and a separate ICESCR covenant were approved;
- 1976 – the covenants entered into force, becoming together with the UDHR the International Bill of Human Rights.

5. Another example is the international criminal law regime:
- 1945–6 Nuremberg tribunals;
- 1946–8 Tokyo trials;
- 1993 Former Yugoslavia tribunal;
- 1994 Rwanda tribunal;
- 1998 International Criminal Court (Rome Statute);
- 2002 ICC actually came into existence.

6. Both timelines illustrate how long it can take to bring projects to fruition when international agreement is needed and influential states such as the US refuse support.

3.1.2 The UN Charter

1. There were proposals to incorporate a bill of rights in the UN Charter and although this was not done:
   a) article 68 provided that ECOSOC would establish commissions in economic and social fields to promote human rights;

    b) the UN Commission on Human Rights was established in 1946.

2. In the Charter there are merely exhortatory references to human rights, and even article 56 in which all Members 'pledge themselves' is an unenforceable obligation.

3. The Preamble, second paragraph, said that the peoples of the UN were determined to reaffirm faith in fundamental rights, in the dignity and worth of the human person, and in the equal rights of men and women and of nations large and small.

4. More important substantive provisions include:

- article 1(3) expresses some of the broad purposes of the UN, including promotion and encouragement of human rights and fundamental freedoms without distinction as to race, sex, language or religion, perceived as being an element of cooperation between states in solving international problems of an economic, social, cultural or humanitarian character;

- article 13(1)(b) refers to the initiation of studies for the purpose of making recommendations into the promotion of international co-operation in the economic, social, cultural, educational and health fields;

- article 55 provides for the promotion of higher standards of living, full employment, economic and social development, with progress and solutions to international economic, social, health, cultural and educational problems, all in order to create stability, wellbeing and peace;

- article 56 reinforces this, members pledging themselves to take joint and separate action in cooperation with the UN to achieve those objectives;

- article 62(2) enables ECOSOC to make recommendations to promote human rights based on studies or reports to be presented to the General Assembly, Member States, and specialised agencies;

- article 68 empowers ECOSOC to set up commissions in the economic and social fields to promote human rights, and such other commissions as may be required for the performance of its functions.

3.1.3 The Universal Declaration of Human Rights

1. The original idea was that the UDHR would be followed by a single convention containing comprehensive provisions that states would ratify, incorporating the:
- civil and political elements in articles 1–21;
- economic and social rights in articles 22–8;
- duties in articles 29 and 30.

2. Ideological differences early in the Cold War prevented this, so in 1952 it was decided to proceed via two separate routes, the ICCPR and ICESCR, agreed in 1966.

3. The UDHR is perhaps the single most important human rights document ever produced because of:
- its timing and global context;
- the influence it has had on subsequent human rights documents and regimes;
- the fact that although it is a declaration and not a treaty, many people believe it has acquired the status of customary international law.

The Preamble

1. This recognised the inherent dignity and inalienable rights of all human beings which need to be based on freedom, justice and peace, and the (then) recent barbarous acts that had outraged mankind's conscience.

2. It also stated that the UDHR would strive to set a common standard of achievement to be brought about by education in order to promote and eventually secure universal recognition and observance of human rights and fundamental freedoms.

Civil and political rights

1. Article 1 states that all humans are born free and equal in dignity and rights, are endowed with reason and conscience, and should act towards each other in a spirit of brotherhood.

2. Article 2 entitles all humankind to the rights and freedoms contained in the Declaration without distinction of any kind, but specifically race, colour, sex, language, religion, political or other opinion, national or social origin, birth or other status.

3. Article 3 says that everyone has the right to life, liberty and security of person.

4. Article 4 prohibits slavery, the slave trade and servitude.

5. Article 5 prohibits torture, cruel, inhuman or degrading treatment or punishment.

6. Articles 6–11 deal with fair trials requiring:
   a) everyone to be recognised as a person before the law;
   b) equality without discrimination before the law;
   c) effective remedy by national tribunals in cases of violation of fundamental rights;
   d) absence of arbitrary arrest, detention or exile;
   f) full equality to a fair and public hearing by an independent and impartial tribunal;
   g) presumption of innocence, guarantee of defence, no retrospective law.

7. Article 12 requires absence of arbitrary interference with privacy, family, home or correspondence.

8. Articles 13–15 grant:
   a) freedom of movement and residence within borders, and the right to leave;
   b) the right to seek asylum from persecution abroad, but not for non-political crimes;
   c) the right to nationality and not arbitrarily to be deprived thereof.

9. Article 16 gives adults the right to marry freely and have a family.

10. Article 17 provides the right to own property solely or jointly, and not arbitrarily to be deprived thereof.

11. Articles 18–20 deal with beliefs and how they can be expressed, meaning freedom of:

a) thought, conscience and religion, and the right both to change and manifest them;
b) opinion and expression, and to seek and impart information;
c) assembly and association without compulsion.

12. Article 21 provides the right to take part in government, to have equal access to public services, and to periodic and genuine elections held by universal and equal suffrage with secret ballots.

13. Article 22 gives the right to social security and the rights that provide dignity and free development of personality, within each state's resources.

Economic, social and cultural rights

1. Article 23 states that everyone has:
   - the right to work;
   - free choice of employment with good conditions;
   - equal pay for equal work:
     a) all so as to provide sufficient remuneration for dignified family existence;
     b) backed up by the right to join a trade union.

2. Article 24 stipulates:
   - reasonable limitation of working hours;
   - sufficient paid holidays to allow for rest and leisure.

3. Article 25 provides for:
   a) an adequate standard of living for health and wellbeing to enable sufficient food, clothing, housing, medical and social services, which should lead to;
   b) security against unemployment, sickness, widowhood, old age and other circumstances beyond the individual's control.

4. Article 26 provides for:
   a) free and compulsory education, at least in the elementary and fundamental stages;
   b) further education generally available and equally accessible to all on merit;

  c) full human development of personality and respect for others, with parental choice.

5. Article 27 allows for free participation in community cultural life and the right to share in artistic and scientific advancement, subject to protection of intellectual property rights.

6. Article 28 states that everyone is entitled to a social and international order in which the rights and freedoms set forth in the UDHR can be realised.

Duties

1. Article 29 states that everyone has duties to the community in which alone the free and full development of personality is possible, but they:
   - must be subject to limitations in so far as they are necessary to secure recognition for the Declaration's rights and freedoms;
   - cannot be exercised contrary to the purposes and principles of the UN.

2. Article 30 provides that nothing in the Declaration can be interpreted to imply that anyone – state, group or individual – is entitled to do anything contrary to the aims and objectives of the UDHR.

Status

1. The then newly-formed UN Commission on Human Rights under the chairmanship of President Franklin D Roosevelt's widow Mrs Eleanor Roosevelt, decided to work towards a declaration rather than a treaty, in order to secure as rapid and widespread approval as was possible at the time, and the fact that it was:
   a) an international UN statement gave it moral and political importance;
   b) less than a treaty but more than a recommendation meant it might grow to become binding under customary international law.

2. It was to:
- include civil, political, economic, social and cultural rights;
- be short and inspirational;
- be almost, but not quite, universally acceptable and accepted.

3.2 UN ORGANS

3.2.1 UN Commission on Human Rights

1. In the UN hierarchy the Commission on Human Rights (the Commission), established in 1946, is inferior to the General Assembly and ECOSOC, but is vitally significant for human rights, having:
- 53 member governments elected for three-year terms by ECOSOC;
- a chairmanship rotating between the main political and geographical groups, sometimes resulting in states with dubious human rights records such as Libya holding the chair.

2. The Commission meets annually in Geneva for a six-week period in March and April and:
- is attended by over 3,000 delegates from member and observer states and NGOs;
- can hold emergency sessions when needed;
- considers approximately 100 resolutions, decisions and statements;
- the Sub-Commission on the Promotion and Protection of Human Rights provides assistance in the form of working groups, experts and rapporteurs.

3. The procedures of the Commission are geared towards:
- examining, monitoring and reporting publicly on the human rights position in particular states (the country mechanisms or mandates);
- monitoring major world-wide violations (thematic mechanisms or mandates).

3.2.2 UN High Commissioner for Human Rights

1. The UNHCHR is the official who heads the UN's human rights efforts, under the leadership of the Secretary-General and subject to the mandates given to him or her by the General Assembly, ECOSOC and the Commission.

2. Appointment is by the Secretary-General subject to approval by the General Assembly, with a four-year term and the possibility of one renewal, and subject to geographical rotation.

3. The position was established in 1993 following the Vienna World Conference on Human Rights, despite a lack of enthusiasm of the then Secretary General Boutros-Ghali, although subsequently Secretary-General Kofi Annan has been more sympathetic to human rights concerns.

4. The responsibilities of the UNHCHR include:
   - promotion and protection of effective enjoyment of civil, cultural, economic, political, and social and developmental rights;
   - provision of advisory and technical services, and financial assistance, to states requesting them;
   - coordination of the UN human rights education and public information programmes;
   - playing an active role in the removal of obstacles to the full realisation of human rights;
   - establishing field presences in sensitive areas from Burundi, Cambodia and Colombia to Guatemala, Mongolia and Togo.

5. The office has been held as follows:
   a) 1994–7 Jose Ayala-Lasso, former Ecuadorean foreign minister;
   b) 1997–2002 Mary Robinson, former President of Ireland;
   c) 2002–3 Sergio Vieira de Mello, former Brazilian and UN diplomat, killed by a bomb in Baghdad;
   d) 2004 Louise Arbour, former Canadian Supreme Court Justice.

3.2.3 Other UN organs with human right involvement

General Assembly

1. Chapter II, article 13, provides that the General Assembly shall initiate studies and make recommendations under paragraph:
   (a) for promoting international political cooperation and development of international law; and
   (b) for promoting international cooperation in the economic, social, cultural, educational and health fields, and assisting in the realisation of human rights and fundamental freedoms for all without distinction as to race, sex, language or religion.

2. The General Assembly usually votes by simple majority and all members are treated equally, having one vote regardless of size or population.

3. Most business is conducted on a consensus basis without necessarily taking votes, although certain matters require a two-thirds majority such as:
   - accession of new members;
   - matters of peace and security;
   - budgetary concerns.

4. The General Assembly is empowered under article 10 to discuss any matters within the scope of the Charter, although the only reference to human rights in the Charter is in article 13.

5. There is no provision for the General Assembly to decide for itself the extent to which it would promote human rights issues, and historically this led to arguments by and disagreements with individual states, such as South Africa when the UN condemned apartheid.

6. Nowadays with the operation of the Commission and the supervision of the UNHCHR responsibilities are clearer, although states are prepared to argue when they are criticised for alleged human rights abuses.

Security Council

1. The Security Council paid little attention to human rights during the Cold War, but it did condemn apartheid, originally raised as an issue by India in 1946.

2. The UN response was the Westphalian attitude that South African citizens of Indian origin were no one else's business.

3. The Security Council only imposed a mandatory arms embargo on South Africa under Chapter VII in 1977, followed by the rejection in 1984 of the white-imposed new constitution.

4. However, over the years the idea of what constitutes threats to peace gradually expanded and there developed an indirect approach to protecting human rights.

5. With the ending of colonialism the Security Council often disagreed about human rights issues with other states represented through the General Assembly.

6. The Security Council has 15 members, ten of which rotate, but is effectively controlled by the five powers who have the veto, ie:
   - Britain;
   - France;
   - China;
   - Soviet Union (now Russia);
   - United States.

7. The Security Council can often stymie human rights by use of the veto, eg the US protects Israel whenever it is criticised for its behaviour towards Palestinians, despite breaches of human rights by both sides.

8. The Cold War inhibited other Security Council actions, now obvious from the increase in post-Cold War UN authorisation of military force since 1990, eg:
   - Iraq;
   - Somalia;
   - former Yugoslavia;
   - Rwanda;
   - Haiti.

9. Other important developments have been the:
   - sanctioning of peace-keeping operations;
   - establishment of the former Yugoslavia and Rwanda genocide tribunals.
10. Another significant trend is that conflicts are now mostly occurring within, rather than between, states.

Social, Humanitarian and Cultural Committee (third committee)

1. The third committee's job is to uphold basic rights and freedoms throughout the world, but in a wider sense than is often understood.
2. Its concerns include:
   - refugees, famine and discrimination;
   - CEDAW;
   - elimination of racism;
   - use of mercenaries;
   - the UN Literacy Decade starting in 2003.

Legal Committee (sixth committee)

1. The sixth committee concerns itself with a wide range of legal matters, many impinging on or requiring involvement in human rights matters, directly or indirectly.
2. Examples include:
   - the ICC;
   - measures to eliminate international terrorism;
   - the International Convention Against the Reproductive Cloning of Human Beings.

Sub-Commission on the Promotion and Protection of Human Rights

1. Between 1947 and 1999 this was known as the Sub-Commission on Prevention of Discrimination and Protection of Minorities, and differs markedly from the Commission itself as it comprises 26 independent experts rather than governmental representatives, who are elected by the commission after nomination by governments.

2. They meet for four weeks a year in August, but also have working groups examining complaints made to the sub-committee.

3. It is a relatively independent and creative body, more pressure group than servant of states, concerning itself with a range of human rights activities including slavery, rape as a weapon in conflicts, and rights of sustenance.

3.3 THE COVENANTS

1. Some of the main shared characteristics between the ICCPR and the ICESCR are:
   a) the language used, emphasising:
      ● in the former, rights expressed in absolute terms;
      ● progressive realisation and availability of resources in the latter.
   b) inter-dependence between the two, both growing out of the UDHR, the:
      ● former from articles 1–22;
      ● latter from articles 23–8.
   c) another example of this can be seen from equivalences between them, eg:
      ● ICCPR article 18: parental right to choose a child's education;
      ● ICESCR article 13: child's right to education and parental right to choose schools;
      ● ICCPR article 22: right to freedom of association;
      ● ICESCR article 8: right to be a member of a trade union.

2. They were dealt with separately because of Cold War differences referred to previously, but as well as ideological confrontation, other reasons for this division were recognised during the drafting stage as including:
   ● large-scale decolonisation in the 1950s;
   ● changing balances of diplomatic and military strength during that period;

● the difficult reality of turning aspirational notions of the UDHR into acceptable binding legal obligations.

3.3.1 ICCPR

The ICCPR contains 51 articles and two optional Protocols.

Part I

1. This contains the first article, stating that all people have the right of self-determination, and so are entitled freely to:
   ● determine their political status;
   ● pursue their economic, social and cultural development.
2. All peoples (plural) are also able freely to dispose of their natural wealth and resources for their mutual benefit, regardless of international economic obligations to cooperate, and under no circumstances should a people be deprived of its own means of subsistence.
3. Self-determination is to be promoted by states and those responsible for non-self governing territories.
4. What article 1 does *not* do, however, is to explain how one determines what is meant by peoples, or a people.

Part II

This part contains articles 2–5, dealing with:

1. Respect within states for all individuals for the rights contained in the covenant without distinction of any kind whether race, colour, sex, language, religion, political or other opinion, national or social origin, property, birth or other status.
2. Adoption by states of the machinery necessary to implement this.
3. The need for state parties to ensure the equal right of men and women to enjoy the civil and political rights contained in the covenant.
4. Limited derogation is allowed in times of public emergency,

but nothing in the covenant is to be interpreted as working against the grain of the document.

Part III

This contains articles 6–27, the heart of the covenant, in summary dealing with:

1. Inherent right to life, freedom from torture, inhuman or degrading treatment, and from slavery, servitude and the slave trade.
2. The right to liberty and security of person, without arbitrary arrest or detention, and humane treatment when deprived of liberty.
3. No imprisonment on civil (ie non-criminal) matters.
4. Freedom of movement and residence within a territory, and no expulsion from a territory without compelling reason, eg national security.
5. Equality before courts and tribunals with fair trials, no retrospective criminal laws, and right of recognition for everyone before the law.
6. No arbitrary or unlawful interference with privacy, family, home or correspondence, freedom of thought, conscience and religion, and the right for everybody to hold opinions without interference.
7. Prohibition of propaganda for war and advocacy of national, racial or religious hatred and incitement to discrimination, hostility or violence.
8. Rights of peaceful assembly and freedom of association, and recognition that the family is the natural and fundamental group unit of society with the right to marry freely.
9. Protection of children without discrimination, and the right to take part in public affairs.
10. Equality before the law, and protection of ethnic, religious and linguistic minorities.

Part IV

1. Article 28 establishes a Human Rights Committee, the remainder of the ICCPR dealing with consequential

organisational and administrative arrangements.

2. The first optional Protocol authorises the Human Rights Committee established under Article 28 to receive and consider communications from individuals claiming to be victims of a violation by a state party.

3. The second optional Protocol abolishes the death sentence for ratifying states parties.

3.3.2 ICESCR

Part I
Article 1 is the only article in part I and is the same as that in the ICCPR.

Part II
Articles 2–5 contain undertakings to take steps, especially economic and technical but within available resources:

a) to guarantee the rights contained in the ICESCR without discrimination, with

b) a proviso for developing countries that they can limit the extent of their commitment to economic rights:

- the states parties undertake to ensure equality between the sexes in respect of economic, social and cultural rights;
- these rights are expressed in terms of resource-constrained objectives, rather than absolute obligations.

Part III
This part contains Articles 6–15, the main substantive provisions, dealing with:

1. Rights to work in just and favourable conditions, to form and join trades union, and to have social security and insurance.

2. Recognition of the family, especially children and young persons.

3. The need for an adequate standard of living including food, clothing, housing and continuous improvement of living conditions.

4. Achieving the highest attainable standard of physical and mental health.

5. Provision of compulsory and free primary education, and education for all to develop fully the human personality and sense of dignity.

6. Allowing broad cultural enjoyment, including the benefits of scientific progress and its applications, and literary and artistic productions.

Part IV
This part deals with submission of reports by states parties, and consequential administrative procedures.

3.4 THE FOURTH TIER

3.4.1 The UN hierarchy

The UN hierarchy comprises a:
- first tier of the UN Charter 1945;
- second tier of the UDHR 1948;
- third tier being the ICCPR and ICESCR approved in 1966 and entering into force in 1977;
- fourth tier consisting of the major UN conventions, of which the following are amongst the most important.

3.4.2 Convention on the Prevention and Punishment of the Crime of Genocide 1951

1. Many states were guilty of genocide during the twentieth century, before and after it was defined as such, including the USSR, China, Germany, Cambodia, Japan and Rwanda.

2. Although what is now called genocide has been perpetrated throughout history, the word itself was coined during the Second World War by the Polish scholar Raphael Lemkin.

3. Genocide comprises two essential elements:
   a) mental, ie the intent to destroy, in whole or in part, a national, ethnical, racial or religious group, as such;

   b) physical, comprising one or more of the following five acts:
- killing group members;
- causing serious mental or bodily harm to group members, eg rape or mutilation;
- deliberately inflicting on group members conditions of life calculated to bring about its physical destruction in whole or in part, eg deprivation of physical resources such as water, blockading food or detention;
- imposing measures intended to prevent births within the group, eg forcible sterilisation or abortion;
- forcibly transferring children of the group to another group.

4. In addition to genocide there can also be, even prior to killing:
- conspiracy to commit genocide;
- direct and public incitement to commit genocide;
- attempt to commit genocide;
- complicity in genocide.

5. 135 states are parties to the Convention, while 52 nations are not, including major states such as Indonesia, Japan and Nigeria.

3.4.3 The Convention on the Elimination of all Forms of Racial Discrimination 1966

1. This is divided into three parts containing 25 articles, with article 1 defining racial discrimination as any distinction, exclusion, restriction or preference based on race, colour, descent, or national or ethnic origin which nullifies or impairs equal recognition, enjoyment or exercise of political, economic, social or cultural human rights and fundamental freedoms.

2. It particularly condemns racial segregation, apartheid and propaganda, and in article 5 guarantees a wide range of rights including:
- equal treatment before tribunals;
- security of person and participation in elections;
- freedom of movement and nationality;

- marriage and choice of spouse;
- property and inheritance;
- freedom of thought, conscience and religion, opinion and expression;
- freedom of assembly and association;
- economic, social and cultural rights;
- work and trades union rights;
- housing, health, education and cultural activities.

3.4.4 Convention on the Elimination of All Forms of Discrimination Against Women 1981 (CEDAW)

1. This Convention:
   a) was adopted by the General Assembly in 1979;
   b) is sometimes regarded as an international bill of rights for women.
2. It comprises a preamble and 30 articles; after defining what is meant by discrimination in this context, it establishes a national agenda for ending it.
3. Discrimination against women is any distinction, exclusion or restriction made on the basis of sex, which has the effect or purpose of impairing or nullifying the recognition, enjoyment or exercise by women, of human rights and fundamental freedoms in the political, economic, social, cultural, civil or any other field.
4. By ratifying the Convention, states accept a number of basic tenets, including:
   - incorporation of sexual equality principles into domestic law;
   - abolition of discriminatory laws and adoption of suitable ones;
   - elimination of discriminatory acts against women by individuals or organisations;
   - establishment of tribunals to protect women;
   - the principle that equality should apply in political and public life, health, education and employment;

- affirmation of women's rights to bear children and to acquire and change nationality for themselves and their children.

5. In March 2004, the Convention had 176 states parties.

3.4.5 Convention Against Torture and Other Cruel, Inhuman and Degrading Treatment or Punishment 1987

1. This entered into force in June 1987 and has 3 parts and 33 articles, the background referred to in the Preamble being:
- UN Charter article 55;
- UDHR article 5;
- ICCPR article 7;
- Declaration on the Protection of All Persons from Being Subjected to Torture and Other Cruel, Inhuman or Degrading Treatment or Punishment adopted by the General Assembly December 1975.

2. Article 1 defines torture as:
- any act by which severe pain or suffering, whether physical or mental, is intentionally inflicted on a person for such purposes as obtaining from him or a third person information or a confession; or
- punishing him for an act he or a third person has committed or is suspected of having committed; or
- intimidating or coercing him or a third person;
- when such pain or suffering is inflicted by or at the instigation of or with the consent or acquiescence of a public official or other person acting in an official capacity;
- but not including pain or suffering arising only from, or inherent in or incidental to lawful sanctions.

3. Under article 2, no exceptional circumstances whatsoever may be invoked to justify torture, and *refoulement* (sending or extraditing to a state where torture is likely to occur) is forbidden by Article 3.

4. Other important provisions are that states must make torture a domestic extraditable crime and arrest suspects, keep interrogation methods, practices and rules under review, and investigate suspicious circumstances.
5. Part II establishes a Committee against Torture comprising ten independent experts to serve four-year terms.
6. States parties must submit reports to the UN through the Secretary General indicating measures taken to fulfil their obligations under the Convention.

3.4.6 Convention on the Rights of the Child 1989

This is divided into three parts, part I, articles 1–41 *inter alia* dealing with the following matters:

- defining a child as every human being under 18 years, unless majority is attained earlier;
- stating that in all actions the interests of the child must be the primary consideration;
- children's inherent rights to life, a name, nationality, identity, and to live with their parents;
- states must prevent illicit transfer and non-return of children;
- due weight must be given to children's wishes, with respect for their rights to freedom of thought, conscience, religion, association and assembly;
- there must be no interference with privacy, family, home or correspondence and access to information, and recognition of parents' common responsibilities;
- there should be protection of children from physical or mental violence, injury or abuse, neglect or negligent mistreatment, maltreatment, exploitation or sexual abuse;
- further articles deal with adoption, refugees, disabilities, health, care proceedings, education and cultural rights, and the right not to be exploited.

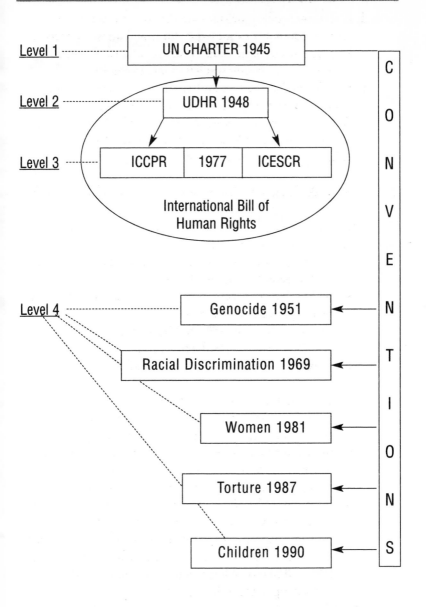

CHAPTER 4

REGIONAL REGIMES

4.1 THE REGIMES

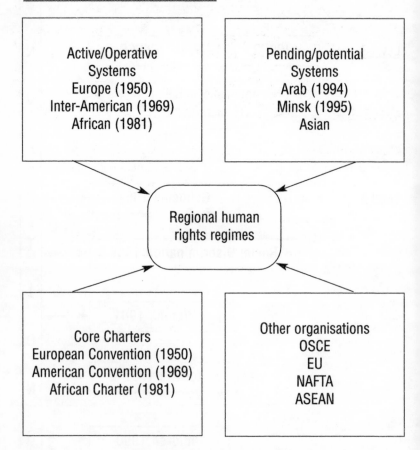

```
┌─────────────────────────┐        ┌─────────────────────────┐
│   Active/Operative      │        │   Pending/potential     │
│        Systems          │        │        Systems          │
│      Europe (1950)      │        │       Arab (1994)       │
│  Inter-American (1969)  │        │      Minsk (1995)       │
│     African (1981)      │        │         Asian           │
└─────────────────────────┘        └─────────────────────────┘
            ↘                                  ↙
                  ┌──────────────────────┐
                  │   Regional human     │
                  │    rights regimes    │
                  └──────────────────────┘
            ↗                                  ↖
┌─────────────────────────┐        ┌─────────────────────────┐
│     Core Charters       │        │   Other organisations   │
│ European Convention (1950)│      │          OSCE           │
│ American Convention (1969)│      │           EU            │
│  African Charter (1981) │        │          NAFTA          │
│                         │        │          ASEAN          │
└─────────────────────────┘        └─────────────────────────┘
```

4.1.1 Active operative regional systems

Contrasting with the universal or global system, there are three regional structures, in descending order of development, effectiveness and sophistication:

- European (1950);
- Inter-American (1969);
- African (1981).

4.1.2 Pending/potential systems

There are other systems not properly effective, yet with potential:
- Commonwealth of Independent States Convention on Human Rights (Minsk) 1995;
- Arab Charter on Human Rights 1994;
- Asian (prospective).

4.1.3 Other organisations

Other organisations play some role in regional and inter-regional human rights affairs, depending on one's definition of human rights, including:
- The Organisation for Security and Cooperation in Europe (OSCE);
- The European Union (EU);
- Association of South East Asian Nations (ASEAN).

4.1.4 Core charters

This chapter concentrates, although not exclusively, on Europe, the Americas and Africa, whose core charters are the:
- European Convention on Human Rights 1950 (an instrument of the Council of Europe);
- American Convention on Human Rights 1969;
- African Charter of Human and People's Rights 1981.

4.2 EUROPE

As this book has three chapters devoted to human rights issues specifically in the UK and Europe, more detail is given here on other regional regimes, although Europe has the most advanced regional system when the scope, influence and effectiveness of its operations is considered.

4.2.1 Principal documents

Within Europe the main charters and conventions are as follows (and care should be taken not to confuse regional conventions with those of the UN):

- Convention for the Protection of Human Rights and Fundamental Freedoms 1950 (together with a number of Protocols extending its provisions) (ECnHRs);
- European Social Charter 1961, with Protocols, revised 1996;
- European Convention for the Prevention of Torture and Inhuman or Degrading Treatment or Punishment 1987;
- European Charter for Regional or Minority Languages 1992;
- Convention on Human Rights and Biomedicine 1997;
- Charter of Fundamental Rights of the European Union 2000.

4.2.2 Convention rights

1. The ECnHRs, or the Convention, came into existence as a result of the establishment of the Council of Europe in 1949, for a number of reasons:
   - reaction to Second World War atrocities and determination to avoid future repetition;
   - to encourage cooperation rather than conflict between European States;
   - to avoid the dangers that arose from the punishment and humiliation inflicted on Germany after the First World War;
   - to establish an effective and enforceable regional agenda, based on the new global regime.
2. The terms were similar to early drafts of the UN Covenant on Civil and Political Rights, but contained no provisions on self-determination or minority group rights.
3. To ensure effective implementation, article 1 requires the parties to secure convention rights to everyone within their jurisdiction.

4. Article 13 requires States to provide an effective remedy before a national authority for everyone whose rights have been violated.

5. Subsequent Protocols were needed to implement provisions that could not be agreed in 1950, including rights relating to:

● property;
● education;
● free elections;
● movement and residence;
● abolition of the death penalty.

6. All 44 states who are members of the Council of Europe are parties to the Convention, whose broad emphasis has tended towards rectifying delay in process and promoting rights of non-interference, compared with concerns about tackling systematic violence and forced disappearances in Latin America.

4.2.3 European Social Charter

1. The emphasis immediately after the Second World War was on civil and political rights and the need to foster and guarantee democracy, so economic and social rights were subsequently recognised in the European Social Charter.

2. There are various Protocols but the system was updated in 1996 by a revised and consolidated charter.

3. This has led to more fragmentation than for the Convention, which all 44 Council of Europe members have ratified.

4. In the case of the Social Charter, 17 members have not ratified any of its provisions or Protocols.

5. The Charter includes employment conditions covering:

● non-discrimination;
● prohibition of forced labour;
● trades union rights and decent working conditions;
● equal pay;

- prohibition of child labour;
- maternity protection.

6. Additionally, 'social cohesion' conditions cover:
- health protection and social security;
- rights relating to families, children and the elderly;
- migrant workers.

4.3 THE AMERICAS

4.3.1 Principal documents

There are a number of important documents to consider here:

a) American Declaration of the Rights and Duties of Man 1948;
b) American Convention on Human Rights 1969 (see below), together with the:
- Additional Protocol to the American Convention on Human Rights in the Area of Economic, Social and Cultural Rights 1988;
- Protocol to the American Convention on Human Rights to Abolish the Death Penalty 1990.
c) Specific conventions:
- Inter-American Convention to Prevent and Punish Torture 1985;
- Inter-American Convention on the Forced Disappearance of Persons 1994;
- Inter-American Convention on the Prevention, Punishment and Eradication of Violence against Women 1994.

4.3.2 The OAS apparatus

1. The Organisation of American States (OAS) originated in the International Union of American Republics of 1890, but was established in its modern form at the 1948 Bogota conference.

2. The 1948 Charter entered into force in 1951, and was subsequently amended by the Protocols of:
- Buenos Aires 1967;
- Cartagena de Indias 1985;
- Washington 1992;
- Managua 1993.

3. It has a number of objectives, including:
- strengthening peace and security on the continent;
- promoting democracy;
- providing for common action against aggression;
- seeking solutions to political, juridical and economic problems.

4. It operates through General Assembly annual meetings, consultation between foreign ministers, and has a General Secretariat and Permanent Council located in Washington DC.

5. The Inter-American Commission on Human Rights was created in 1959, leading to the Convention in 1969, which entered into force in 1978.

6. In Latin and South America the political climate has been very different from that of Europe, with unelected military governments being the norm until recently, so there has been more concern than in Europe over torture, disappearances and corrupt judiciary.

7. There are 35 OAS member states, 25 having ratified the Convention and 20 having recognised the jurisdiction of the Court.

4.3.3 American Declaration of the Rights and Duties of Man 1948

1. This pre-dates the UN Universal Declaration and European Convention, but did not in itself establish the American regime and supervisory apparatus; its content is similar to the Universal Declaration, including economic and social rights.

2. There are also ten articles setting out the responsibilities and duties of the citizen, eg to:
● obtain education for himself and his children;
● vote;
● render civil and military service to his country.

4.3.4 American Convention on Human Rights 1969

1. This is the treaty based on the above declaration, sometimes referred to as the Pact of San Jose, Costa Rica. It:
● followed the Third Special Inter-American Conference in Buenos Aires in 1967;
● approved the incorporation into the Charter of the Organisation broad standards for economic, social and educational rights, thus differing from European arrangements.
2. Additionally, there are specific articles covering the right to:
● juridical personality (article 3);
● a name (article 18);
● nationality (article 20).
3. There is also a right of reply (article 14), and rights of the child (article 19).
4. The American Convention contains specific rights to:
● property, incorporated in article 21 rather than by Protocol;
● freedom of movement and residence (article 22);
● participate in government (article 23);
● equal protection of the law (article 24);
● judicial protection by the laws (article 25).
5. Chapter III contains only one article (26) whereby states undertake to adopt internal and international progressive measures to achieve the full realisation of the rights implicit in the economic, social, educational, scientific and cultural standards of the OAS Charter.
6. The additional 1988 Protocol introduced obligations relating to:

- non-discrimination (article 3);
- the right to work and to have just, equitable and satisfactory conditions of work with trade union rights (articles 6, 7 and 8);
- further rights to social security and health in articles 9 and 10;
- a healthy environment by article 11.

7. These supplementary provisions also included:
  - food and education (articles 12 and 13);
  - the benefits of culture under article 14;
  - protection of the family, children, elderly and handicapped (articles 15, 16, 17 and 18 respectively).

8. The 1990 Protocol addresses abolition of the death penalty; if and when adopted and ratified by American States it will not under article 2 allow any reservations, but would not extend to war-time or extremely serious crimes of a military nature.

4.3.5 Inter-American Convention on the Forced Disappearance of Persons (1994)

1. Forced disappearance abuses of human rights were endemic in Latin and South America for much of the twentieth century, so this treaty was essential.

2. The Preamble said that OAS members were:
  - disturbed by the persistence of the forced disappearance of persons, which affronted the conscience of the hemisphere;
  - concerned at violations of numerous non-derogable and essential human rights in the American and UN Declarations, and in the American Convention.

3. They undertook not to practise or tolerate forced disappearances, defined in Article II as having four essential elements:
  a) depriving persons of their freedom in whatever way;
  b) perpetration by or with the support of the state;

    c) absence of information and refusal to acknowledge
       occurrences;

    d) impedance or negation of legal and procedural remedies.

4. Forced disappearances could not be treated as political
offences and criminal prosecutions would not be subject to
statutes of limitation, ie they could be prosecuted at any
time in the future, with no defence of superior orders.

5. War, threats of political instability, or other public
emergencies, would not justify the crime, and:

- detainees should be held in an officially recognised
establishment;

- they should be brought before properly constituted
judicial authority without delay;

- states must provide mutual assistance to search for, trace
and identify victims.

4.3.6 Comparisons

1. The American regime is more complex than the European
system, being based on the Declaration and Convention.

2. It is more ambitious than the European Convention because
the Inter-American Commission:

- hears cases;

- makes visits;

- prepares country reports on the human rights position of
member states.

3. Stemming from different continental political histories,
violations in Europe tend to be individual rather than
collective, often because of procedural incompetence eg
delay in providing hearings and solutions, whereas in the
Americas there have been repeated and large-scale gross
violations.

4. There is no enforcement procedure in the Americas and
decisions are not necessarily accepted as legally binding; in
Europe the Committee of Ministers guarantees remedial
action.

4.4 AFRICA

4.4.1 Principal documents

The main African documents are the:

a) 1981 African Charter, containing 68 articles, divided into Rights and Duties, Measures of Safeguard, and General Provisions;

b) 1998 Protocol on the Establishment of an African Court on Human and People's Rights containing 35 articles;

c) OAU Convention Governing the Specific Aspects of Refugee Problems in Africa 1969, with 15 articles and concerned with refugees, asylum, prohibition of subversion, non-discrimination and connected matters in the African context;

d) African Charter on the Rights and Welfare of the Child 1990 dealing with freedoms, education, protection against abuse, responsibilities and organisational matters.

4.4.2 The OAU apparatus

1. The Organisation of African Unity (OAU) was until recently the regional body of the African states, having 53 states parties, the Charter of the OAU being adopted in 1963.

2. In 1981 the Assembly of Heads of States and Government of the OAU adopted the African Charter on Human and People's Rights, coming into force in 1986.

3. There was only one implementation instrument, the Commission, with no enforcement provisions, so its scope was more limited than in Europe or the Americas.

4. The emphasis was on inviolability of borders, one of the main African characteristics having been reluctance to promote human rights or take effective action when violations occurred.

5. The First OAU Ministerial Conference on Human Rights met in April 1999 in Mauritius, issuing an impressive

Declaration and Plan of Action, but in 2002 it was disbanded and a new African Union (AU) organisation was launched in Durban, South Africa, to replace the OAU.

6. Critics claim that in 39 years of existence the OAU did little to protect the human rights of African citizens; it remains to be seen whether the AU can do better, considering the pandemic continental problems.

4.4.3 The African Union

The AU structure is broadly modelled on the EU, so is not primarily a human rights organisation although possessing some human rights machinery, the organisation comprising the:

a) Assembly, made up of members' heads of state with functions including common policies, membership, and conflict resolution;

b) Executive Council, ie the foreign ministers of its members whose functions include foreign trade, social security, food, agriculture and communications;

c) Permanent Representative Committee consisting of the Ambassadors to the AU whose function is to prepare the work for the Executive Council;

d) Commission (Secretariat), Specialised Technical Committees, Pan-African Parliament, Economic, Social and Cultural Council, and three Financial Institutions.

4.4.4 AU Human Rights bodies

The two AU bodies possessing a human rights focus are:

a) the Court of Justice;

b) the Peace and Security Council, with 15 members responsible for monitoring and intervening in conflicts, to be advised by a Council of Elders with an African force at its disposal.

The Court

1. In mid-2004 it was predicted that the Court might be established by 2005, a year later than envisaged.
2. It will have one permanent and ten temporary members, with procedural rules to be established.
3. The court's location has not been agreed, suggestions including Senegal, South Africa and Ethiopia, where the AU is based, as the OAU was originally established there at the invitation of the late Emperor Haile Selassie.

The Peace and Security Council

1. The first practical steps towards the council were taken in February 2004 in Libya with agreement to establish a 15,000 strong peace-keeping force divided into five regional brigades, the 'African Standby Force', but it is likely to comprise existing military units of individual states earmarked for action as required.
2. It is roughly modelled on the UN version, but without power to decide independently on military or humanitarian intervention, although it may be allowed to commence 'peace support operations' and send observers to trouble spots.
3. Moammar Gadaffi's radical idea that there should be a pan-African army was rejected by other AU leaders.
4. The EU has pledged about $US300 million towards it but African contributions are already problematical.

4.5 THE MINSK CONVENTION

1. The Commonwealth of Independent States Convention on Human Rights (Minsk) 1995 was:
   - opened for signature in May 1995;
   - originally signed by Armenia, Belarus, Georgia, Kyrgyzstan, Moldova, Russia and Tajikistan;
   - subsequently ratified by the Russian Federation, Tajikistan and Belarus;

- entered into force in August 1998.
2. The control mechanism comprises the CIS Commission on Human Rights, which monitors practice by issuing recommendations, the members of the Commission being appointed representatives of the states parties.
3. The CIS Convention does not offer as extensive protection as the European Convention, and the Council of Europe is concerned that difficulties might arise for states such as Russia, which are now subject to both Conventions.
4. Particular worries arose about the submission of individual applications to the European Court of Human Rights, as the Council of Europe believes that the CIS Commission cannot offer equivalent protection to the European Court, nor are its recommendations enforceable.
5. Some states subject to the CIS Convention cannot aspire to membership of the Council of Europe, so they at least have some regional safeguards in place, albeit less satisfactory than for Europe.

4.6 ARAB CHARTER ON HUMAN RIGHTS

4.6.1 The Charter

1. Although largely inactive, this is a Charter of the Council of the League of Arab States, and the Preamble:
   a) refers to the Arab world as the birthplace of civilisation and cradle of religions;
   b) rejects racism and Zionism;
   c) acknowledges the eternal principles of brotherhood established by the Islamic Shari'ah and other divinely-revealed religions;
   d) expresses belief in the rule of law;
   e) reaffirms the principles of the UN Charter and the International Bill of Human Rights, together with the Cairo Declaration on Human Rights in Islam 1990.

2. It is divided into four parts, the first comprising one article split into two which:
   a) proclaims the right of all peoples to self-determination, free choice of political structure, and to pursue their economic, social and cultural development;
   b) condemns and argues for elimination of racism, Zionism, occupation and foreign domination.
3. Part II comprises articles 2–39, characterised by succinctness and simplicity.
4. They include protection rights derived from the UN Declaration, eg:
   - Life, liberty and security of person protected by law (article 5);
   - Presumption of innocence until guilt is proved by lawful trial with defence guarantees (article 7);
   - No application of the death penalty for political offences (article 11);
   - No citizen to be expelled from his own country, or prevented from returning (article 22);
   - Right to own private property (article 25);
   - Eradication of illiteracy and the right to education (article 34).
5. Part III deals with administrative matters relating to the Committee of Experts, tasked with considering reports submitted by the 22 member states parties, and Part IV with ratification.

4.6.2 The Cairo Declaration on Human Rights in Islam 1990

1. This was the Arab world's precursor to their Charter, reinforcing the UN documents, issued following a conference in Cairo in 1990.
2. The Declaration is similar to a charter, containing the Preamble and 25 articles, and issued to serve as general guidance for member states in the field of human rights following a report of legal experts.

3. It is expressed in Islamic religious terms, referring to the human family descended from Adam, subordinate to Allah, with life being a God-given gift.

4. It addresses a variety of rights which as well as the family include:
   - humanitarian concerns;
   - sexual equality;
   - prohibition of colonialism;
   - freedom of work and movement;
   - ownership of physical and intellectual property;
   - security, equality and freedom from hostage taking.

5. It concludes by asserting that:
   a) authority is a trust;
   b) abuse or malicious exploitation thereof is prohibited;
   c) all rights and freedoms stipulated in the Declaration are subject to the Islamic Shari'ah, the only source of reference for explanation or clarification of any of its articles.

4.7 ASIA AND ASEAN

4.7.1 Asia

1. While the Arab Charter exists but is not actively operative, equivalent Asia regional human rights do not yet exist.

2. The Arab human rights documents are cultural rather than universal, and perhaps Asia is too large and culturally diverse to allow equivalence.

3. Some Asian pundits dispute universal rights:
   - one view is the culturally relativist approach that one size does not fit all;
   - but this may be special pleading without moral authority when expressed by oppressive regimes.

4. Given the continent's religious diversity, tolerance and freedom of choice would need to be central to any regional regime.

5. The future of Asian human rights is unclear but might be established through an existing organisation such as the Association of Southeast Asian Nations (ASEAN).

4.7.2 ASEAN

1. This body was founded by non-communist states in Bangkok in 1967 to promote economic, social and cultural cooperation and strengthen regional peace.
2. The founding members were:
   * Thailand, Singapore, Malaysia, Indonesia, the Philippines and Brunei;
   * they were later joined by Vietnam, Laos, Burma and Cambodia;
   * the total population is now 530 million with a combined gross domestic product of 600 billion Euros.
3. ASEAN+3 allows for cooperation with China, Japan and South Korea, and other bodies include:
   * ASEAN Regional Forum (ARF);
   * Asia–Pacific Economic Cooperation (APEC);
   * South Asia Association for Regional Cooperation (SAARC);
   * Shanghai Organisation for Cooperation (comprising China, the Russian Federation, Kazakhstan, Kyrgyzstan, Tajikistan and Uzbekistan).
4. Some ASEAN activities could become the focus of regional human rights development, eg:
   a) the Policy Initiative for the Establishment of an ASEAN Human Rights Mechanism;
   b) some States have internal rights machinery, eg the:
      * Thai Parliamentary human rights standing committee;
      * national human rights commissions in Indonesia and the Philippines.
5. Little progress has been made towards establishing a credible Asian regime, with various reasons being suggested:
   * states may regard human rights as an internal matter;
   * cultural relativism, rejecting universalism as an

inappropriate Western concept;
- a view that collective security, economic and social interests take precedence over individual rights;
- the size and diversity of the continent.

4.8 THE ORGANISATION FOR SECURITY AND COOPERATION IN EUROPE (OSCE)

1. The Organisation for Security and Cooperation in Europe (OSCE) asserts a low-profile diplomatic process whose basic purpose is to pre-empt and prevent conflict in three areas:
   a) human;
   b) politico-military;
   c) economic/environmental.
2. It has 55 participating states spanning a geographical area from Vancouver to Vladivostok, so covering four major regions:
   a) continental Europe;
   b) the Causcasus;
   c) Central Asia;
   d) North America.
3. Unlike the UN it has no status under international law, so its decisions are not legally enforceable but rely on political recognition.
4. The OSCE was launched in Helsinki in 1972, emerging through a series of processes to the Final Act, the 1992 Helsinki Document establishing the basis for the OSCE's Office for Democratic Institutions and Human Rights (ODIHR), sited in Poland with a specific human rights mandate to assist participating states to:
   a) ensure full respect for human rights and fundamental freedoms;
   b) abide by the rule of law;
   c) promote principles of democracy and to build, strengthen and protect democratic institutions;

  d) promote tolerance throughout society.
5. Functions of the ODIHR include:
   a) promotion of democratic elections;
   b) practical support in consolidating democratic institutions;
   c) human rights training for governments and civil society;
   d) helping participating states to implement international legal obligations and OSCE commitments on terrorism in line with human rights principles;
   e) promotion of Roma and Sinti issues.

4.9 THE EUROPEAN UNION (EU)

1. It is important not to confuse the EU with the Council of Europe's human rights regime, but the EU itself is concerned with human rights and claims to be world leader in regional human rights protection.
2. The entry into force of the 1993 Treaty on European Unity (TEU) advanced integration of human rights and democratic principles in EU policies, emphasising consolidation of democracy and the rule of law.
3. The 1999 Treaty of Amsterdam inserted a new article 6 in the TEU reaffirming that:
   a) the EU is founded on principles of liberty, democracy, respect for human rights and fundamental freedoms, and the rule of law;
   b) serious and persistent violation of those principles would lead to suspension of some state rights under the Union Treaty.
4. The Treaty of Amsterdam incorporated other human rights dimensions including:
   a) a clause to combat discrimination;
   b) measures concerning asylum, refugees and immigration;
   c) provisions relating to employment, working conditions and social protection.
5. The Nice Summit in 2000 proclaimed the EU Charter of Fundamental Rights, codifying materials from various

sources including the European Convention on Human Rights, international instruments and common constitutional traditions.

6. The EU fosters human rights in other ways, eg:
   a) the Luxembourg Declaration of 1991 and the 1998 Declaration on the fiftieth anniversary of the Universal Declaration;
   b) human rights clauses in over 50 bilateral trade and cooperation agreements;
   c) funding activities, eg assisting the AU.

CHAPTER 5

THEMES

5.1 INDIGENOUS PEOPLES

1. The UN has estimated that there are some 300 million people inhabiting large areas of the globe who can be described as indigenous or aboriginal, who are:
- descendants of the original inhabitants of a country or geographical area who were there prior to external settlement or colonisation;
- nearly always dominated by latecomers through conquest, occupation, settlement or otherwise.

2. Examples of indigenous peoples include:
- Mayas of Guatemala and Aymaras of Bolivia;
- Inuit and Aleutians of the circumpolar region (formerly called Eskimos);

- Saami of Northern Europe;
- Aborigines of Australia and Maoris of New Zealand.

3. The problems of indigenous people demonstrate the fundamental and universal aspects of human rights, involving among other things:
- culture;
- economics;
- political rights;
- social security;
- fair treatment.

4. American Indians first approached the League of Nations for help in the 1920s, but nothing was done until 1970 when the Sub-Commission on Prevention of Discrimination and Protection of Minorities recommended a study should be undertaken, the final report being made in 1984.

5. It dealt with various human rights matters including:
- defining what is meant by indigenous peoples;
- the role of government and NGOs;
- establishing basic human rights principles;
- specific areas of action including health, education, housing, language, culture and legal institutions.

6. In 1982 the Economic and Social Council set up the Working Group on Indigenous populations which has two formal tasks, to:
- a) review national developments pertaining to the promotion and protection of rights and freedoms of indigenous peoples;
- b) develop international standards concerning their rights, taking account of similarities and differences in their situations and aspirations throughout the world.

7. The Working Group produced a draft rights declaration, which was submitted to the Commission on Human Rights for consideration, resulting in the International Decade of the World's Indigenous People 1995–2004.

8. In May 2002 a Permanent Forum on Indigenous Issues was established with a mandate to address indigenous issues relating to:

- economic and social development;
- culture;
- the environment;
- health and education;
- human rights.

5.2 ABOLITION OF SLAVERY

5.2.1 Background

1. The history of slavery is almost as old as the history of mankind, and slavery still exists in the world, despite national and international abolition.
2. The English entered the slave trade in 1562 when a cargo of slaves was taken from Sierra Leone by Sir John Hawkins and sold in St Domingo.
3. Charles II gave a charter to a company that took 3,000 slaves per year to the West Indies, and other charters followed.
4. In 1770 Britain was responsible for over half the 100,000 slaves being transported from West Africa per year, and by 1791 the trade involved more than 160 ships and 5,500 sailors.

5.2.2 Abolition

1. In 1776 the first Parliamentary motion against slavery was introduced by David Hartley, and William Wilberforce began his crusade in 1787, suffering many defeats in trying to overcome entrenched economic interests that relied on slavery.
2. He introduced annual motions in the House of Commons for abolition of the slave trade up to the year 1800, despite the unpopularity it caused him.
3. This led to the Abolition of the Slave Trade Act 1807, but it only abolished the trade, not slavery itself.

4. America and Denmark followed suit, with other states – France, Spain and the Netherlands – being unable to trade because of the wars taking place at this time, although Portugal's slave trade continued.

5. A renewed Anti-Slavery Society was formed in 1823, members including Henry Brougham and William Wilberforce.

6. The Slavery Abolition Act 1833 provided that former slaves were to serve an apprenticeship to their previous masters of seven years:
   - the taxpayer compensated former masters with a total of £20 million sterling;
   - the Bishop of Exeter received compensation of £12,700 for his 665 slaves.

5.3 ABOLITION OF THE DEATH PENALTY

1. The death penalty has been the ultimate punishment or sanction since prehistory, used in different ways, eg:
   - as a crude form of terror;
   - imposing discipline on society through judicial execution;
   - as a means of coercing citizens, eg forcing them to take up arms;
   - belief that it acts as a deterrent.

2. In humanitarian law, the Geneva Conventions, by common article 3:
   a) codify customary international law;
   b) prohibit sentencing and executions without guaranteed previous judgments of a properly constituted court.

3. Global human rights documents recognise the right to life, as the:
   a) UDHR 1948 proclaimed the right to life;
   b) ICCPR 1966:
      - set out the principle that no one should be arbitrarily deprived of life;

- said that where the death penalty has not been abolished, it should only apply to the most serious crimes;
  c) 1989 Protocol to the ICCPR abolished the death penalty in peacetime.
4. Regional provisions include the:
   a) European Convention 1950, under which no one was to be deprived of life intentionally apart from court sentence following conviction of (impliedly) serious crime;
   b) American Convention on Human Rights 1969, reflecting the terms of the 1966 UN Covenants, later supplemented by an additional protocol.
5. Despite widespread abolition, capital punishment is still carried out by some regimes, eg the United States, China, Saudi Arabia and various African states.
6. Although the trend has been towards abolition over the last 60 years or so, it is possible that the majority of people do not agree, believing it either to be a deterrent or the right punishment for serious transgression.
7. Arguments in favour of abolition include the following:
   - people are wrongly convicted and mistakes made are irrevocable;
   - it is not a deterrent, even though this might appear contrary to common sense;
   - it allows no element of repentance, redemption or reform;
   - it comprises revenge as much as punishment or protection for society.

5.4 THE RULE OF LAW

1. The purpose of the rule of law is to legitimise government by showing that it is impartial, fair and must be obeyed, whether or not you agree with a particular political regime or specific provisions.
2. The essence of the rule of law is that authority is subject to and constrained by law, comprising the following elements:

- no one should be punishable except for distinct breaches of the law;
- no one is above the law;
- everyone should be subject to the jurisdiction of the ordinary courts (*Entick v Carrington* (1765));
- punishment should be in the ordinary courts and in the manner prescribed by law;
- there should be no arbitrary or random exercise of power;
- discretionary exercise of power is common in modern government but its extent should be clearly defined.

3. Where there is no written constitution:
   - there should be judicial review of administrative action;
   - constitutional principles are contained in the common law and a few legislative provisions, such as Magna Carta (1215) and the Bill of Rights (1689).

4. The incorporation of most of the European Convention by the Human Rights Act 1998 provides additional support for the rule of law.

5. The rule of law does not stand in isolation, and is analogous and connected to other rights principles:
   - accused persons should not be placed in double jeopardy;
   - all people should be treated equally, eg no separate rights of trial for certain individuals, such as peers;
   - everyone is innocent before the law until proved guilty;
   - law, especially criminal law, should not be retrospective;
   - there should be separation between executive (governmental) and judicial functions, part of the doctrine of the separation of powers;
   - the content of law should be clear and readily accessible;
   - everyone should have access to affordable legal advice and representation.

6. Prior to the:
   a) European Convention;
   b) right of individual application to the European Commission; and

c) enactment of the Human Rights Act;
- judicial review was an important part of the direct application of the rule of law to protect human rights in the UK, eg where a:
- compulsory purchase order was wrongly made, adversely affecting citizens' property rights (*White and Collins v Minister of Health* (1936));
- mother wanted to challenge provisions that undermined her view of family life (*Gillick v West Norfolk and Wisbech Area Health Authority* (1985).

7. The rule of law has come under strain in recent years because of perceived terrorist threats, especially regarding:
- detention without trial;
- curtailment of legal aid;
- restriction of jury trial;
- imposition of double jeopardy.

5.5 GENOCIDE, CRIMES AGAINST HUMANITY AND WAR CRIMES

5.5.1 Background

1. Genocide was the term invented during WW2 to define a crime committed by mankind for countless generations.
2. The roots of the post-Second World War genocide regime grew out of the First World War because:
- genocide, although not then named as such, had been committed by the Turks against the Armenians during that war;
- this led to bilateral and multilateral treaties after the Great War, attempting to prevent repetition;
- unsuccessful attempts were made to try German leaders for war crimes, and later to establish an International Criminal Court;
- no substantial distinction had been made between what

are now defined separately as crimes against humanity
and genocide.

3. In the Second World War, more determined efforts were
made to address the problem and in 1943 specific steps were
taken, including:
   - establishing the UN Commission for the Investigation of
   War Crimes;
   - issuing the Moscow Declaration referring to evidence of
   atrocities, massacres and mass executions.

4. After the war, the allies agreed that states must be held
responsible for atrocities committed against their *own*
populations, and 'atrocities' became in due course 'crimes
against humanity', which included:
   - murder;
   - extermination;
   - enslavement;
   - deportation and other inhuman acts committed against
   civilian populations.

5. The Agreement for the Prosecution and Punishment of
Major War Criminals of the European Axis and Establishing
the Charter of the International Military Tribunal was
adopted by the four major allies, the US, UK, France and
Russia, in August 1945, and 19 other states accepted the
treaty while playing no part in the trials.

6. In the Nuremberg trial of the major war criminals:
   - 24 were indicted;
   - 19 were convicted;
   - death sentences were imposed in 12 cases.

5.5.2 The modern position

1. The groups protected by the UN Convention on the
Prevention and Punishment of the Crime of Genocide are:
   - national;
   - racial;
   - ethnical;
   - religious.

2. Groups excluded from protection include:
   - political;
   - ideological;
   - linguistic;
   - economic.
3. This is problematic, as many horrific events are outside the definition, resulting in attempts being made to:
   a) include within the definition events that are not, thus risking discrediting the Convention;
   b) extend the boundaries of the definition.
4. These crimes invoke the notion of 'group rights', compared with a usual core feature of Western rights that they are individual and personal.
5. Genocide can be committed in many ways, eg:
   - killing;
   - causing serious bodily or mental harm;
   - inflicting conditions of life calculated to bring about physical destruction;
   - imposing measures intended to prevent births;
   - forcibly transferring children.
6. Crimes against humanity can be committed by:
   - murder;
   - deportation or forcible transfer of population;
   - imprisonment or other severe deprivation of physical liberty;
   - torture;
   - rape, forced prostitution, pregnancy or sterilisation;
   - enforced disappearance of persons;
   - apartheid;
7. War crimes arise in varying contexts, eg:
   - torture;
   - inhuman treatment or biological experiments;
   - destruction and appropriation of property;
   - denying a fair trial;
   - unlawful deportation and transfer;
   - hostage taking, attacking civilians or civilian objects.
8. Some actions may be both crimes against humanity and war crimes.

5.6 HUMANITARIAN INTERVENTION

1. Humanitarian intervention can be defined as armed intervention by one or more states in another state's affairs, without that state's agreement, with the intention of preventing actual or threatened humanitarian disaster, especially when caused by widespread human rights violations.

2. The four essential elements are:
   a) genuine humanitarian intention;
   b) actual and severe breaches of human rights;
   c) breach of sovereignty of the state being invaded;
   d) armed intervention.

3. Article 24(1) and Chapter VII of the UN Charter give the Security Council power to take measures necessary to restore international peace and security, and with this authority humanitarian intervention is possible and legal.

4. By article 24(1), members:
   - confer on the Security Council primary responsibility for the maintenance of international peace and security;
   - agree that in carrying out its duty under this responsibility the Security Council acts on their behalf;
   - concede that the justification provided by the article is to ensure prompt and effective action by the UN.

5. Chapter VII comprises articles 39–51 inclusive of the Charter and covers:
   - actions threatening peace;
   - actual breaches of the peace;
   - acts of aggression.

6. Whenever such action is contemplated, in addition to article 24(1) and Chapter VII, article 2 of the Charter also needs to be considered, as it:
   - proclaims principles of sovereign equality;
   - requires good faith in carrying out obligations;
   - insists on settlement of international disputes by peaceful means without risking peace, security and justice;

- disallows threat or use of force against territorial integrity or political independence of other states;
- says that nothing contained in the Charter authorises the UN to intervene in matters that are essentially within the domestic jurisdiction of any state.

7. The state sovereignty doctrine is important, as it provides the main inhibition on stronger states taking advantage of weaker ones, so all breaches of sovereignty are potentially dangerous to stability.

8. There is in-built conflict or instability, therefore, between leaving well alone and interfering to protect people or redress perceived wrongs, requiring a balance between sovereignty and human rights.

9. There is not presently a recognised regime in force clearly stating what the ground rules should be for humanitarian intervention, but possible criteria include:
- threat or occurrence of serious and extensive human rights violations;
- adequate proven evidence of this with an urgent need to act;
- refusal to remedy or prevent the violations;
- limitation of action to removing the threat or preventing abuse;
- extensive support for the action from victims and neighbours;
- force only used as a last resort with no breaches of the laws of war, and a good chance of success;
- clear and unambiguous UN authority, and a post-conflict restoration plan.

10. These considerations are vital to:
- maximise support and legitimacy;
- minimise damage and adverse consequences;
- uphold human rights.

11. In the 1990s there were a number of interventions that involved some humanitarian rationalisation, eg:
- Kosovo;
- East Timor
- Sierra Leone.

12. Since the end of the Cold War, the question has arisen of whether a group of states with authority falling short of the above criteria is justified in undertaking humanitarian intervention, and whether it can be used as a fall-back reason when previously stated justifications fail.
13. Steps short of intervention can be used, including:
    - criticism by governments, organisations, NGOs and INGOs;
    - diplomatic pressure;
    - economic sanctions;
    - supplying aid and humanitarian assistance.

5.7 APARTHEID

5.7.1 South Africa

1. This Afrikaans word was first used by Jan Smuts in 1917, two years before he became Prime Minister of South Africa:
   - its literal translation is 'aparthood';
   - properly translated into English this means apartness or separation.
2. Today it means a legally sanctioned system of ethnic segregation such as existed in South Africa between 1948 and 1990.
3. It is antithetic to primary norms of human rights universality, and negates or denies provisions of instruments such as the International Bill of Human Rights.
4. Apologists for the system claim that it prevents minority races from being swamped by numerically superior races, and if properly applied allows fair treatment of all sectors of society.
5. In practice it contravenes legal and human rights norms because it:
   a) produces a hierarchy of races;
   b) enforces by law widespread segregation on society, eg for:
      - work;
      - marriage;

- where people can live;
- c) arrogates to the ruling class and race the bulk of the State's resources and assets.
6. South Africa suffered many adverse effects, eg:
   - non-whites were excluded from national government and full voting rights;
   - they were not allowed to operate businesses in white-only areas;
   - they comprised 70 per cent of the population but were confined to small segregated parts of the country and forced to carry passes;
   - workers and their families were separated, with public transport and other facilities being segregated;
   - their land was inferior and their townships squalid;
   - in virtually all aspects of their lives, blacks were kept away from and under inferior conditions to whites.
7. Apartheid was introduced in South Africa after the National Party won the 1948 general election. The racial legislation included:
   - Prohibition of Mixed Marriages Act 1949;
   - Reservation of Separate Amenities Act 1953;
   - Bantu Education Act 1953;
   - Black Homeland Citizenship Act 1971.
8. Increasing protests throughout the 1950s eventually led to the Sharpville demonstration against the Pass Law (requirement to carry identity cards) in March 1960 where police killed 69 demonstrators and injured 180.
9. UN General Assembly Resolution 1761 was passed on 6 November 1962 condemning apartheid and calling on other states to terminate military and economic relations with South Africa.
10. Nelson Mandela was sentenced to life imprisonment in 1964 and South Africa gradually became more isolated while repeated resolutions passed at the UN condemned racism, including World Conferences Against Racism in 1978 and 1983.

11. In 1984 some reforms were instituted and when F W de Klerk succeeded P W Botha as president in 1989 the end was in sight, the ban on the ANC being lifted in 1990, Mandela being released from prison, and repeal of the remaining apartheid laws.

12. In 2003 President Thabo Mbeki announced that 660 million rand (US$85 million) would be used to recompense approximately 22,000 people who had been tortured, imprisoned or who had lost relatives during the apartheid era.

5.7.2 The UN Convention on Apartheid

1. The International Convention on the Suppression and Punishment of the Crime of Apartheid:
   - was adopted and opened for signature and ratification by General Assembly resolution 3068 (XXVIII) of 30 November 1973;
   - comprised 19 articles and entered into force in accordance with article XV on 18 July 1976.

2. Article I declares apartheid to be a crime against humanity, as well as violating principles of international law and the UN Charter, and under article II the commission of inhuman acts that come within the definition of the crime include:
   a) denial to a member or members of racial groups the right to life and liberty of person by:
      - murder;
      - infliction of serious bodily or mental harm;
      - arbitrary arrest and illegal imprisonment.
   b) deliberate imposition on a racial group of living conditions calculated to cause it or their physical destruction in whole or in part;
   c) legislative and other measures calculated to prevent racial groups from participating in the political, social, economic and cultural life of the country;

d) any measures designed to divide the population along racial lines:
- by creating reserves or ghettos;
- prohibiting mixed marriages;
- expropriating property belonging to racial groups.

3. Other articles address:
- international criminal responsibility;
- amendment of state laws;
- trial by competent tribunals;
- submission of periodic reports and supervision by the Commission on Human Rights;
- exclusion of these crimes from political designation so as to avoid extradition.

5.8 TRUTH COMMISSIONS

1. Commissions of Inquiry are used for many purposes; out of these have grown truth commissions in at least 25 states from Argentina to Zimbabwe, and although they differ markedly from one place and purpose to another, they tend to have a number of features in common which include:
- researching and reporting on human rights abuses over particular turbulent periods in states where the rule of law has broken down;
- taking evidence from survivors, relatives and perpetrators about what happened in a forum which is outside the usual state judicial apparatus;
- reaching conclusions as to fact and making a final report containing recommendations to prevent future recurrence of abuses;
- bearing the authority of the state's current regime, sometimes established with the assistance of international organisations.

2. They vary considerably with regard to:
- precise mandate terms;
- processes and procedures adopted;
- the use made of conclusions.

3. One of the earlier modern examples was the commission set up in Argentina following the Falklands War, not directly because of the war, but because defeat led to the removal of military government and a desire to find out about previous misuse of power.

4. The National Commission on the Disappeared was:
   - established by President Raul Alfonsin in 1983 and comprised ten members;
   - published in September 1984, reporting on 9,000 disappearances occurring during military rule from 1976–1983.

5. Perhaps the best known is the South African Commission set up in 1995 by the South African parliament to investigate human rights abuses during apartheid between 1960 to 1994:
   - its chairman was Archbishop Desmond Tutu and it had 17 members, holding public meetings throughout South Africa;
   - the amnesty committee processed over 7,000 applications by perpetrators, and in return for confessions they were granted immunity from prosecution;
   - the reparation and rehabilitation committee recommended appropriate compensation, with the final report being presented to President Nelson Mandela in October 1998.

6. After the reunification of Germany, a 27-member Study Commission for the Assessment of History and Consequences of the SED Dictatorship in Germany:
   - was established by the German parliament in 1992;
   - investigated human rights violations under communist rule between 1949 and 1989.

7. One of the principal reasons for having truth commissions rather than criminal trials is to achieve 'closure' for survivors and relatives by finding out the truth, rather than convicting a few perpetrators.

8. Other truth commissions that have been relatively successful in achieving their objectives are Chile and El Salvador, but

not all results are satisfactory, eg:

- The Guatemalan conflict was brought to an end but the commission's terms were extremely narrow;
- Uganda failed to complete theirs because of lack of funding and political will.

9. Truth Commissions may operate strictly within states' own frameworks, but they nearly all draw heavily on global human rights norms and are further characterised by:

- real desire for change;
- the need to resolve issues and put the past behind them;
- the need to address issues of amnesty, forgiveness and compensation.

CHAPTER 6
EUROPEAN HUMAN RIGHTS

6.1 THE BEGINNINGS

Failure of the League of Nations

War crimes

Division of Europe by the Iron Curtain

Need to reconstruct

COUNCIL OF EUROPE

European Convention on Human Rights

6.1.1 Post-Second World War Europe

1. European regional human rights began after the Second World War.

2. Germany was divided into zones between the four main allies: the US, USSR, France and the UK.

3. Eastern Europe was dominated by the Soviets and kept under tight control, Hungary and Czechoslovakia being invaded when they stepped out of line.

4. Western Europe was relatively free, but opposing ideologies led to nearly 50 years of 'Cold War'.

5. The two power blocs reorganised themselves into defensive alliances in light of the new circumstances, the West forming NATO and the East the Warsaw Pact.

6. The war left huge reconstruction problems, with aid provided by the Americans under the Marshall Plan in 1947 to start the process.

7. The Organisation for European Cooperation was established in 1948.

6.1.2 The legacy of war crimes

1. Nazi atrocities during the war caused the allies to institute war crimes tribunals at Nuremberg and Tokyo, the former being established by the Charter of the International Military Tribunal in August 1945.

2. The allies tried and punished by death or imprisonment a number of individuals under three main categories:
   a) crimes against peace;
   b) war crimes;
   c) crimes against humanity.

3. One problem was that at the time that murderous acts were perpetrated during the war, it was not thought that states could commit crimes against their own citizens.

4. The principles of international law established by the Military Charter and judgment were adopted in 1950 by the International Law Commission of the United Nations.

5. The Tokyo trials were heavily criticised as being more akin to victor's justice than were the Nuremberg trials.

6. Some of the atrocities were so egregious that new descriptions or categories had to be invented, including the term genocide, coined by Ralph Lemkin in 1943.

6.1.3 The European response

1. One reason for the failure of the League of Nations was lack of support by influential nations, but another significant factor was that human rights were ignored by the League.
2. The allies determined that the new global regime, the United Nations, would avoid this mistake, so human rights comprised a vital ingredient in the organisation and its organs.
3. As both world conflicts originated in Europe, many European states believed that in addition to the UN there had to be a specific European response, concentrating on human rights.
4. During 1948–9, international negotiations led to the founding of a new organisation to encourage peace and good relations over and above short-term self-interested political, economic and military objectives, to be achieved by a Committee of participating government ministers with a consultative assembly, which eventually became the Council of Europe whose statute was signed in London on 5 May 1949.

6.1.4 The British response

1. The British government supported the organisation and idea of a Convention to encourage human rights in Europe, but did not think it was necessary for the UK to become too closely involved because:
   - they considered that the common law was superior to continental civil law;
   - common law remedies such as *habeas corpus* and jury trial were felt to be adequate to protect citizens;
   - they failed to understand the end of the empire and the need for closer ties with Europe.
2. Britain therefore initially decided against allowing its citizens to bring complaints before the newly established Commission on Human Rights.

6.2 THE COUNCIL OF EUROPE

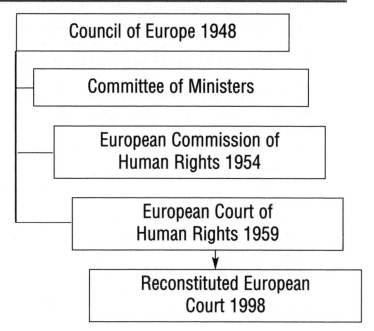

6.2.1 Council of Europe institutions

1. The Congress of Europe met in The Hague in 1948 to establish the Council of Europe, with objectives that included:
   - upholding the rule of law;
   - fostering human rights;
   - drafting a charter of human rights.
2. The three main institutions of the Council of Europe were the:
   - European Commission on Human Rights, established in 1954;
   - European Court of Human Rights, established in 1959 and reconstituted in 1998, sitting in Strasbourg;
   - Committee of Ministers of the Council of Europe, whose members are the foreign ministers of the 44 member states.

3. The Council of Europe is distinct from the European Union (EU), formerly known as the Common Market and the European Economic Community (EEC).

6.2.2 Development of European Human Rights

1. The Committee of Ministers meets six times a year to ensure that the Court's judgements are carried out (article 46, amended by Protocol 11).
2. The ministers' or their deputies' other duties include reviewing various aspects of human rights such as:
   - anti-racism;
   - abolition of the death penalty;
   - reformation or up-dating of the Convention.
3. Prior to 1998, the *Commission* decided on admissibility of human rights applications, but because the system was slow, overloaded and generally unsatisfactory, the *Court* was reconstituted and became full-time in November 1998, now dealing with admissibility and substantive hearings (Protocol 11).
4. The Court has the same number of judges as there are member states (currently 44), but there is no rule that every state must be represented by a judge.

6.3 EUROPEAN CONVENTION PRINCIPLES

6.3.1 Characteristics of the Convention

Basic facts about the Convention are:

- It has international treaty status and its full title is the Convention for the Protection of Human Rights and Fundamental Freedoms;
- Signed in November 1950, it entered into force September 3, 1953;
- The emphasis is on individual and political rights rather than collective economic, social and cultural rights;
- These tend to represent western ideas of personal freedom as opposed to:
  a) Soviet bloc economic and social objectives (in Cold War terms); or
  b) Third World aspirations of developmental, educational or health rights.

6.3.2 UK involvement

1. The UK was one of the founding members and played a crucial role in drafting the treaty, but omitted to incorporate it into UK law in 1953.
2. The Labour Party made an electoral commitment in 1997 to introduce the Convention into domestic law and to 'bring rights home'.
3. The Human Rights Act was passed in 1998 and came into effect in October 2000 to allow direct enforcement without having to take cases to Strasbourg, although this still remains an option once domestic routes are exhausted.

6.4 TYPES OF CONVENTION RIGHTS

```
┌─────────────────────────────────────────┐
│   European Convention of Human Rights    │
│        and Fundamental Freedoms          │
│                  1951                     │
└─────────────────────────────────────────┘
              │
        ┌──────────────────────────────────┐
        │            Section I             │
        │       Rights and Freedoms        │
        └──────────────────────────────────┘
              │
        ┌──────────────────────────────────┐
        │           Section II             │
        │  Establishment of the European   │
        │      Court of Human Rights       │
        └──────────────────────────────────┘
              │
        ┌──────────────────────────────────┐
        │           Section III            │
        │     Miscellaneous Provisions     │
        │          Ratifications           │
        │           Derogations            │
        └──────────────────────────────────┘
              │
           ┌──────────────────┐
           │   13 Protocols   │
           └──────────────────┘
```

6.4.1 Categories of rights and reservations

There are a number of categories of Convention rights:
   a) Absolute rights, ie articles 2, 3, 4(1) and 7;
   b) Special rights, ie articles 4(2), 5, 6, 9(1) and 12, together
      with Protocols 1, articles 2 and 3, and Protocol 6 Article 1;

c) Qualified rights, comprising the remainder, ie articles 8, 9, 10 and 11;

d) Derogations and reservation.

6.4.2 Absolute rights

1. These are the most strongly protected rights, not to be restricted even in times of emergency or war.

2. There are, however, special provisions dealing with the death penalty and capital punishment, as unanimity could not be reached on those matters.

3. Apart from these, public interest cannot be used to curtail or interfere with these basic rights, even including action against terrorism or organised crime (*Selmouni v France* (1999)).

4. The four absolute rights are:
   - prohibition against torture;
   - prohibition against slavery and forced labour;
   - no punishment without law;
   - the right to life.

5. Only the prohibition against torture or inhuman or degrading treatment is absolutely unqualified, but even those are open to interpretation.

6. The apparently absolute right to life is qualified by Convention provisions acknowledging exceptions of:
   - self-defence;
   - arrest;
   - prevention of escape from lawful custody;
   - quelling riots or insurrection.

7. The prohibition of slavery and forced labour is qualified by Convention provisions recognising work required during:
   - lawful imprisonment;
   - military service (or conscientious objection alternatives);
   - work required to counter emergencies;
   - disaster work recognised as comprising part of normal civic obligations.

8. The absolute requirement of 'no punishment' without law is slightly qualified in that:
   a) it must not prejudice trial and punishment of people for acts or omissions which, when committed, were criminal according to general principles of law recognised by civilised nations;
   b) it guards against retrospective criminal laws and prevents heavier sentences being imposed than applied when the offence was committed (*Welch v UK* (1995));
   c) if changes are foreseeable as in progressive attitudes to marital rape, the qualification will not apply (*SW v UK* (1995)).

6.4.3 Special rights

1. These are rights which are not quite so strongly protected but which can be restricted in emergency and war situations, and so cover:
   - prohibitions on forced labour (as opposed to slavery);
   - rights to liberty and security;
   - fair trial;
   - freedom of thought, conscience and religion;
   - marriage;
   - education;
   - free elections;
   - abolition of the death penalty.
2. These rights are special because there is justification within the text of the Convention for them to be restricted in the public interest, but only to the extent provided by the Convention.

6.4.4 Qualified rights

1. For qualified rights, private and public interest has to be balanced, which varies between states, so the kinds of right included are:

- respect for private and family life;
- manifesting religion or belief, (as opposed to holding such views);
- freedom of expression, assembly and association;
- protection of property.

2. In order to qualify these rights, any restriction(s) imposed must be:
- prescribed by law;
- legitimate;
- necessary and proportionate;
- not discriminatory.

6.4.5 Derogations and reservations

1. Derogation occurs under article 15 of the Convention when a state withdraws from specified obligations because of war or other public emergency, but only so far as allowed by the exigencies involved.

2. It is not allowed in respect of:
- the right to life;
- freedom from torture;
- slavery and servitude;
- retrospective criminal penalties.

3. It has been used by the UK for the Anti-Terrorism, Crime and Security Act 2001 and for detention of alleged terrorists in Northern Ireland, when:
   a) the European Court found against Britain in *Brogan v UK* (1988)), so the government enacted the Prevention of Terrorism (Temporary Provisions) Act 1989;
   b) the derogation itself was challenged, and that challenge failed (*Brannigan v UK* (1993)).

4. High Contracting Parties can enter reservations (as opposed to derogations) to particular aspects of international treaties, the UK having done so in respect of the educational rights contained in Protocol 1 article 2.

5. The reservation was that the government would only observe the principle so far as it was compatible with the provision of efficient instructions and training and the avoidance of unreasonable public expenditure.

6. Under s16 of the Human Rights Act, designated derogations cease to have effect after five years in UK domestic law unless they are renewed, but this does not apply to reservations.

6.5 OPERATING PRINCIPLES OF THE EUROPEAN COURT

6.5.1 Purposive approach and proportionality

1. The European Court cannot operate legislatively or overrule the treaty, but takes a purposive or teleological approach to interpretation which may be seen as:
   a) broader than the literal rule;
   b) a development of the mischief and golden rules.

2. The advantage is that it has been able to react to changing conditions in Europe over the last 50 years.

3. Because of the wide scope of the Convention and diversity of national cultures, the Court utilises the principle of 'proportionality' in reaching decisions, maintaining a balance between individuals' rights and legitimate State interests.

4. So, it has been held that:
   a) customs officers were not justified in seizing and refusing to return motor vehicles where the owners had evaded payment of duty on alcohol and tobacco (*Lindsay v Commissioners of Customs and Excise* (2002));
   b) such action was disproportionate and failed to distinguish between commercial/professional smugglers and people bringing goods into the UK for personal or family use.

5. Proportionality arises because some individual rights are qualified rather than absolute, eg:

a) article 8(1) states that 'everyone has the right to respect for his private and family life, his home and his correspondence', but,

b) article 8(2) stipulates that there should be no interference by a public authority with the exercise of this right, except in accordance with law and necessary in a democratic society in the interests of the:
   - economic wellbeing of the country;
   - prevention of disorder or crime;
   - protection of health or morals;
   - protection of the rights and freedoms of others;
   - national security;
   - public safety.

6. So in *Handyside v UK* (1976) it was said that every 'formality', 'condition', 'restriction' or 'penalty' imposed, where qualified rights were said to be 'necessary in a democratic society', had to be 'proportionate to the legitimate aim pursued' (paragraph 49).

6.5.2 Margin of appreciation

1. The 'margin of appreciation' doctrine allows states discretion in the extent to which they implement Convention measures:

a) the basis of the doctrine being an acceptance that national bodies, governmental or judicial, are better placed than an international court to determine local needs;

b) the Court not always insisting on strict or narrow interpretation of individual rights, although this doctrine does not apply in domestic law (*R v DPP ex parte Kebilene* (1999)).

2. It is somewhat analogous to the EU principle of subsidiarity.

3. It will not always apply, however: *Goodwin v UK* (2002) involved violations of transsexuals' rights under articles 8 (privacy) and 12 (marriage), and the Court held that current international attitudes towards acceptance of transsexuals meant that states had to adapt their behaviour, which the UK had failed to do.

4. The Convention has been interpreted to impose negative as well as positive responsibilities on states, so rights of peaceful assembly are not merely preventative duties on states but may amount to positive enabling duties (*Plattform 'Artze fur Leben' v Austria* (1988)).

6.6 OTHER EUROPEAN CONVENTIONS

1. Other European Conventions deal with human rights, and the most important are detailed below.

2. The European Convention for the Prevention of Torture and Inhuman or Degrading Treatment or Punishment 1987 has 23 articles and two Protocols added in 1993:

  ● it establishes a European Committee empowered to visit and examine the treatment of imprisoned persons with a view to protecting them from inhuman or degrading treatment or punishment;

  ● it thus extends the provisions in the Convention on Human Rights and requires co-operation from competent national authorities;

  ● the Protocols deal with administrative matters, and this Convention's machinery strengthens article 3 of the Human Rights Convention.

3. The European Charter for Regional or Minority Languages 1992 and the Framework Convention for the Protection of National Minorities 1995 complement each other and are important because of Europe's ethnic diversity:

  ● the former has 23 articles, article 3 requiring states to identify and specify regional or minority languages;

  ● the objectives and principles in article 7 provide practical means to make the Convention effective, eg facilitating minority speech in public life;

- part III provides measures addressing educational, judicial, administrative and public authorities, media and cultural activities, together with economic and social life.

4. The 1995 National Minorities Framework promotes conditions necessary for national minorities to maintain and develop their own cultures, including religion, language, traditions and cultural heritage (article 5).

5. The European Convention on the Exercise of Children's Rights 1996 applies to children under 18 years of age, granting procedural rights to ensure their best interests are observed before judicial authorities:
   - the judicial authority's role is specified, with duties to act speedily to protect children;
   - a Standing Committee is established in Chapter III to keep relevant questions about the Convention under review.

6. The Convention for the Protection of Human Rights and Dignity of the Human Being with regard to the Application of Biology and Medicine, usually known as the Convention on Human Rights and Biomedicine 1997, breaks new ground including human genome, scientific research and organ and tissue removal from living donors for transplanting purposes:
   - article 28 recognises that there are controversial and rapidly advancing issues within the Convention's ambit, so that public discussion is essential;
   - the 1998 Protocol prevents human cloning with no derogation, and the 2002 Protocol protects people's dignity and identity with regard to transplantation of organs and tissues of human origin.

Convention opened for signature
at Rome 4/11/50

UK signed 4/11/50

UK ratified 8/3/51

Convention entered into force
with 10 ratifications 3/9/53

European Commission
created in 1954

Limited Court created 1959

Protocol 11 abolished commission
and allowed individual access 5/11/94

Reconstituted Court
instituted 1/11/98

Human Rights Act 1998
came into effect 2/10/2000

7.1 THE CONVENTION ARTICLES

7.1.1 Rights protected

1. The Convention for the Protection of Human Rights and Fundamental Freedoms 1950 (the European Convention on Human Rights) covers a wide range of measures, summarised below.

2. Section 1 contains the rights and freedoms in articles 2–18 and specifically:

   a) articles 15–8 cover:
      - derogation in times of emergency;
      - restrictions on political activity of aliens;
      - prohibition of abuse of rights;
      - limitation on the ability to restrict rights;

   b) Article 13 gives the right to an effective remedy but it was not incorporated by the Human Rights Act 1998 because:
      - it was thought the Act itself provides all the protection needed;
      - of government fear of giving excessive power to the judiciary.

3. The Convention identifies rights to:
   - life (article 2);
   - liberty and security (article 5);
   - fair trial (article 6);
   - respect for private and family life (article 8);
   - freedom of thought, conscience and religion (article 9);
   - expression (article 10);
   - freedom of assembly and association (article 11);
   - marry (article 12);
   - effective remedy (article 13) although this is not incorporated in UK domestic law.

4. Other rights are expressed as prohibitions against:
   - torture (article 2);

- slavery and forced labour (article 3);
- punishment without law (article 7);
- discrimination on any ground such as sex, race, colour, language, religion, political or other opinion, national or social origin, association with a national minority, property, birth or other status (article 14).

7.1.2 Right to life article 2

1. Everyone's right to life is protected by law subject to qualifications of:
   - judicial execution;
   - self-defence;
   - effecting lawful arrest or preventing unlawful escape;
   - lawful action to quell riot or insurrection.
2. The case of *A (Children) Conjoined Twins: Surgical Separation* (2001) held that an operation to separate twins which would result in certain death of one would not be unlawful, as she would die anyway and it was the only way the other could survive.
3. There is no correlative right to die *R (Pretty) v DPP* (2002 HL), and subsequently in the European Court, where a mentally competent but physically incapable woman was refused an assurance that her husband could legally help her to die.
4. In an earlier case, the Commission declared inadmissible a husband's application to prevent his wife from obtaining an abortion, the life of the unborn foetus being considered more closely connected to the mother.
5. States bear a positive obligation to take appropriate steps to:
   a) safeguard the lives of those within their jurisdiction (*Mahmut Kaya v Turkey* (2000));
   b) take reasonable steps to prevent suicide while in custody (*Keenan v UK* (1998)).

7.1.3 Prohibition of torture article 3

1. There is an unqualified prohibition against subjection to torture or to inhuman or degrading treatment or punishment.

2. Torture is defined in *Ireland v UK* (1978) as deliberate inhuman treatment causing very serious and cruel suffering:
   - inhuman treatment is less severe but may include threats of torture, psychological harm, and physical assault;
   - the behavioural threshold is lowered if the complainant is in custody;
   - degrading treatment is punishment arousing in the victim feelings of fear, anguish and inferiority capable of debasing the victim or breaking his or her moral resistance;
   - vulnerability of the victim is a relevant factor.

3. The European Court held in *Ireland v UK* that Northern Ireland security forces' techniques did not amount to torture, but did constitute inhuman treatment that was also degrading ie:
   - forcing victims to stand against walls for long periods;
   - hooding suspects;
   - subjecting them to noise, sleep, food and drink deprivation.

4. In *Tyrer v UK* (1980) birching a 15-year-old boy in humiliating circumstances breached Article 3.

5. Imposing additional punishment on a prisoner and insufficient monitoring of his known mental condition leading to his suicide was inhuman and degrading treatment and breached article 3 (*Keenan v UK* (2001)).

7.1.4 Freedom from slavery article 4

1. Article 4 says that no one shall be held in slavery or servitude, or be required to perform forced or compulsory labour, with the following exemptions:
   - work done while in detention;

- military service;
- work exacted in times of emergency or calamity threatening life or the wellbeing of the community;
- work or service forming part of normal civic obligations.

2. Neither slavery nor servitude are defined by the European Convention, but the 1926 Slavery Convention defines slavery in article 1(1) as the status or condition of a person over whom any or all of the powers attaching to the right of ownership are exercised.

3. Servitude was explained in *Van Droogenbroek v Belgium* (1982) as the obligation to provide another with services (and) the obligation on the part of the 'serf' to live on another's property with the impossibility of changing his condition.

4. In that case, a 30-year-old convicted thief was sentenced (in addition to two years' imprisonment) to being placed at the Government's disposal for 10 years, but his claim was rejected by the European Court.

7.1.5 Right to liberty and security article 5

1. This right is limited, the operative words being that everyone has the right to liberty and security of person (and) no one shall be deprived of his liberty;

2. Specified exceptions include:
   - lawful arrest and imprisonment in a variety of circumstances;
   - detention to avoid spread of disease;
   - arrest of persons of unsound mind, alcoholics, drug addicts and vagrants.

3. The circumstances listed in article 5 are exhaustive and cannot be added to (*Ireland v UK* (1980)).

4. Ideas of political correctness change over time, so detention of vagrants may now be inappropriate.

5. Distinguishing between deprivation of liberty and restrictions on freedom is difficult, involving degree or

intensity rather than nature or substance (*Guzzardi v Italy* (1980)).

6. In *Steel v UK* (1999) the European Court considered several English cases where there had been detention and conviction for breaches of the peace and held that these were offences within article 5(1)(c), so the arrests were lawful and not in contravention of article 5.

7. In contrast, the applicants in *Hashman and Harrup v UK* (2000) ruined a fox hunt by blowing a false horn to distract the hounds and the:

    a) Crown Court said that they had behaved in a manner *contra bonos mores* (against good standards of behaviour), binding them over to keep the peace even though there had been no actual breach of the peace;

    b) European Court said that such vagueness was not a procedure prescribed by law as no one could predict what standards of good behaviour a future court might expect.

7.1.6 Right to a fair trial article 6

1. The description 'fair *trial*' is a misnomer because the article refers to the determination of civil rights and the obligations of a criminal charge within a reasonable time and by an independent and impartial tribunal established by law, so 'fair *hearing*' might be preferable.

2. The article establishes other essential criteria for fairness such as public pronouncement of verdicts and decisions, and presumption of innocence, although secrecy is allowable where the following justifications apply:

- morality;
- public order;
- national security;
- protection of juveniles;
- protection of parties' private lives.

3. Minimum rights are specified for everyone charged with a criminal offence including:
   - the right to be informed of the nature of the accusation promptly in a language that he can understand;
   - provision of adequate time and facilities to prepare a defence;
   - the ability to defend oneself either in person or with legal assistance;
   - examination of witnesses and use of interpreter services, if needed.

4. Legitimate reasons for excluding the public from hearings include:
   - sexual offences against children (*X v Austria* (1965));
   - divorce (*X v UK* (1977));
   - medical patients' privacy (*Guenoun v France* (1990)).

5. Nevertheless, the basic rule is that:
   a) courts should sit in public unless and until a legitimate reason for privacy arises (*Diennet v France* (1995));
   b) exceptions must be justifiable and proportionate (*Schuler-Zgraggen v Switzerland* (1993)).

6. To ensure fairness, parties should usually be present in court when civil rights and obligations are to be determined, particularly when factual or personal issues have to be resolved, eg *X v Sweden* (1959).

7. 'Equality of arms' means maintaining a balance between the prosecutor and accused, eg providing legal aid or translation services to ensure that a defendant is not unfairly prejudiced by the power and resources of the prosecution.

8. The same principle applies to civil proceedings although the requirements of fairness are less strict as parties are more likely to be equally balanced (*Dombo Beheer v Netherlands* (1993)).

9. Other important elements of fair hearings are that:
   a) there should be no undue delay, everyone under article 6(1) being entitled to a fair and public hearing within a reasonable time;

    b) in assessing reasonableness the court considers the:
- conduct of the applicant and relevant authorities;
- complexity of the case;
- importance of the matter to the applicant.

10. Avoiding delay is important for:
- children (*H v UK* (1987));
- employment disputes (*Nibbio v Italy* (1992));
- cases involving serious personal injuries or old age (*Dewicka v Poland* (2000)).

7.1.7 No punishment without law article 7

1. This article aims to prevent the creation of retrospective offences and increased penalties, and is connected to Protocol 7 dealing with double jeopardy, although the UK has not ratified this.
2. The avoidance of retrospectivity applies both to legislation and the common law (*SW and CR v UK* (1995)).
3. Article 7(2) qualifies the rules by saying that the trial and punishment of any person for acts or omissions which, when committed, were criminal according to general principles of law recognised by civilised nations, enables novel criminal misbehaviour to be punished, the principle deriving from Nazi war crimes made choate after the war.

7.1.8 Right to respect for private and family life article 8

1. Article 8 declares that everyone has rights to respect for private and family life, home and correspondence, without interference by public authority, except such as is in accordance with law and necessary in a democratic society in the interests of the:
- economic wellbeing of the country;
- prevention of disorder or crime;
- protection of health or morals;

- protection of the rights and freedoms of others;
- national security;
- public safety.

2. It is thus considerably qualified, and connected to marriage rights under article 12.

3. Family life is not restricted to marriages, so unmarried couples bound together by children may qualify (*Kroon v Netherlands* (1994)), and other factors for consideration are:
   - whether the parties live together;
   - how long their relationship has lasted;
   - the extent to which they have demonstrated mutual commitment (*X and Y & Z v UK* (1983)).

4. Children play in important part in family life and:
   a) previous ties remain even if the parents have separated (*Keegan v Ireland* (1994));
   b) potential ties must be considered, eg between father and illegitimate child (*Soderback v Sweden* (1998)).

5. Distinctions are drawn between family and private life, so stable relationships between gay or lesbian couples may be recognised as comprising private if not family life in differing contexts, eg where there is a:
   a) partner threatened by deportation (*X and Y v UK* (1983));
   b) claim to inherit a tenancy (*S v UK* (1986)).

6. Besides partners and children, family life can extend to:
   - siblings (*Moustaquim v Belgium* (1991));
   - uncles (*Boyle v UK* (1994));
   - grandparents (*Bronda v Italy* (1998));
   - questions of access and custody (*Hendriks v Netherlands* (1983));
   - maintenance payments (*Logan v UK* (1996));
   - care proceedings (*L v Finland* (2000)).

7.1.9 Right to marry article 12

1. Article 12 is related to Article 8, and says that men and women of marriageable age have the right to marry and

found a family, according to the national laws governing the exercise of this right.

2. Marrying is the means of establishing a legal relationship, so:
   - it does not require cohabitation or procreation;
   - public authorities are not entitled to prevent persons kept in custody, even under life sentence, from marrying (*Hamer v UK* (1979));
   - but prisoners are not currently afforded the right to found a family.

3. The right to marry does not mean that there is a right to divorce (*Johnston and others v Ireland* (1986)), although:
   - parties are free to separate and not be obliged to live together (*Airey v Ireland* (1979));
   - there should not be unreasonable restrictions on divorcees preventing them from remarrying (*F v Switzerland* (1987)).

4. The right to marry is also recognised under article 23 of the International Covenant on Civil and Political Rights.

7.1.10 Freedom of thought, conscience and religion article 9

1. Rights to freedom of thought, conscience and religion includes freedom to:
   a) change religion;
   b) manifest it in worship, teaching, practice and observance.

2. These freedoms are subject only to such limitations as are prescribed by law and necessary in a democratic society in the interests of protecting:
   - public order, health or morals;
   - rights and freedoms of others;
   - public safety.

3. There is an absolute right to freedom of thought, conscience and religion as these are internal matters and cannot practically be restricted, but the freedom to *manifest* them is qualified because of the above restrictions.

4. There is a wide range of rights (not restricted to traditional religious views) protected by article 9 included in the following (chronological) list:
- pacifism (*Arrowsmith v UK* (1978));
- Scientology (*X and Church of Scientology v Sweden* (1979));
- Islam (*Ahmad v UK* (1982));
- Druidism (*Chappell v UK* (1987));
- Jehovah's Witnesses (*Hoffman v Austria* (1993));
- veganism (*X v UK* (1993));
- the Krishna Movement (*Iskon v UK* (1994)).

5. Views not coming within the scope of the article include:
- political beliefs (*McFeeley v UK* (1980));
- pure altruistic ideals (*Vereniging Rechtswinkels Utrecht v Netherlands* (1986)).

6. The 'manifestation' aspects are important because they can cause disharmony, so qualifications preclude:
- convincing one's neighbour of one's beliefs (*Kokkinakis v Greece* (1993));
- giving conscientious objectors the right to avoid military service by alternative activities (*N v Sweden* (1984));
- conscientious objection to observance of municipal obligations such as being bound by planning restrictions (*Iskon v UK* (1994)) or making maintenance order payments *Karakuzey v Germany* (1996)).

7. A careful balance is needed when the question of proselytism arises, between the interests of the would-be converter and the potential convertee (*Kokkinakis v Greece* (1993) *supra*).

7.1.11 Freedom of expression article 10

1. Extends to freedom to hold opinions or receive and impart information and ideas without interference by public authority and regardless of frontiers.
2. It does not prevent states from requiring licensing of broadcasting, television or cinema enterprises.

3. Qualification of this freedom is justified in article 10 because its exercise carries with it duties and responsibilities, so it may be subject to such formalities, conditions, restrictions or penalties as are prescribed by law and necessary in a democratic society in the interests of:
   - national security, territorial integrity or public safety;
   - prevention of disorder or crime;
   - protection of health or morals;
   - protection of the reputation or rights of others;
   - preventing disclosure of information received in confidence;
   - maintaining the authority and impartiality of the judiciary.

4. Expression includes rights to:
   - free speech;
   - press freedom;
   - receive information and find out about things via diverse media including radio, television, film, telephone, and the web;
   - protection for people doing this, eg by journalists not revealing sources and professional persons maintaining client confidentiality.

5. Freedom of expression is important because it is a prerequisite for the enjoyment of other rights and freedoms, and is thus widely interpreted to cover various kinds of expression, political and artistic, commercial, public and private.

6. Case law exemplifies this, eg:
   - allowing questioning of (but not denying) the existence of historical events such as the holocaust (*Lehideux and Isorni v France* (1998));
   - protesting against other people's activities, even where this might involve some interference, eg blood sports (*Hashman and Harrup v UK* (2000));
   - preventing attempts to hold secret inquiries into matters of public concern, such as the Shipman murders (*R (Wagstaff) v Sec of State for Health* (2001));

- press freedom to report celebrity events (*Douglas v Hello!* (2001));
- the right of prisoners to communicate with the press (*R (Simms) v Secretary of State for the Home Dept* (2000)).

7. The media can use public interest to justify matters published, and if acting in good faith, are entitled to rely on the truth of quotations and extracts from other apparently reliable sources, such as official reports.

7.1.12 Freedom of assembly and association article 11

1. Freedom of peaceful assembly and association with others includes the right to form and join trades unions for protection, with no restrictions to be placed on such freedoms other than as prescribed by law and necessary in a democratic society in the interests of:
   - national security or public safety;
   - prevention of disorder or crime;
   - protection of health or morals;
   - protection of the rights and freedoms of others.

2. Under article 11, states can impose lawful restrictions on the exercise of rights:
   - by members of the armed forces;
   - by police;
   - in the course of state administration.

3. These freedoms are connected to and are extensions of article 10 rights to freedom of expression, and assemblies can include:
   a) marches and demonstrations (*Christians Against Racism v UK* (1980));
   b) being in locations where obstruction might be occasioned such as the public highway (*Rassemblement Jurassien and Unite Jurassiene v Switzerland* (1979) and *Jones & Lloyd v DPP* (1999)).

4. Provided that restrictions imposed are lawful, necessary and proportionate, it is legitimate for states to restrict the right

to peaceful assembly in order to:

a) prevent the occurrence of disorder (*Choherr v Austria* (1993));

b) ban meetings and marches in extreme circumstances, provided they are not complete banning orders (*Rai and others v UK* (1995)).

5. With regard to the right of association, other established rules are that:

- political parties come within its scope (*United Communist Party of Turkey v Turkey* (1998));

- prisoners (*McFeeley v UK* (1980)) and professional regulatory bodies (*Revert v France* (1989)) usually will not;

- political activities of state security forces such as the police are acceptable so long as this is in the public interest (*Rekvenyi v Hungary* (1999)).

7.1.13 Obligation to respect human rights (article 1) and Right to an effective remedy (article 13)

Both these fundamental rights are excluded from the HRA, as the enactment itself satisfies article 1 and the courts' ability to provide a remedy for Convention breaches under s8 of the Act is thought to satisfy article 13.

7.1.14 Prohibition of discrimination article 14

1. This article's comprehensive and unqualified provisions state that the enjoyment of the rights and freedoms set forth in the Convention shall be secured without discrimination on any ground such as sex, race, colour, language, religion, political or other opinion, national or social origin, association with a national minority, property, birth or other status.

2. Under the *eiusdem generis* interpretive rule, protection is not restricted to these categories because of the use of the words 'such as' and 'or other status', the latter applying to:

- imprisonment;
- conscientious objection;
- marital and professional status;
- trades union activities;
- illegitimacy.

3. Comparisons must be fair and equivalent, judicial decisions stating that:
   - it is not discrimination to treat married and unmarried couples differently as they have different status (*Lindsay v UK* (1986));
   - trainee barristers are different from trade apprentices (*Van der Mussele v Belgium* (1983));
   - justification that discrimination is in the public interest must be convincing (*Larkos v Greece* (1999));
   - mere administrative convenience for the state will not succeed (*Darby v Sweden* (1990)).

4. Discrimination particularly disliked by the judiciary includes:
   - race (*East African Asians v UK* (1973));
   - denial of sexual equality (*Abdulaziz and others v UK* (1985));
   - illegitimacy (*Inze v Austria* (1987));
   - religion (*Hoffmann v Austria* (1993));
   - nationality (*Gaygusuz v Austria* (1996)).

5. Positive discrimination may be acceptable, eg:
   a) the *Belgian Linguistic Case* (1968);
   b) tax legislation favourable to women to persuade them into employment (*Lindsay v UK* (1986)).

6. The rights encompassed by article 14 are available in conjunction with the other Convention rights rather than being separate and self-standing.

7.2 THE CONVENTION PROTOCOLS

7.2.1 The Protocols

All states were not ready to accept everything in 1950, so some elements were promulgated by later Protocols, including:

- rights to property, education and free elections (Protocol no 1 articles 1, 2 and 3);
- prohibition of imprisonment for debt (Protocol no 4 article 1);
- freedom of movement, prohibition of expulsion of nationals and collective expulsion of nationals (Protocol no 4 articles 2, 3 and 4);
- Protocol 6 dealing with the death penalty;
- Various provisions in Protocol no 7 on criminal appeals, compensation, double jeopardy and equality between spouses.

7.2.2 Protection of property Protocol 1 article 1

1. Protocol no 1 provides that every natural and legal person (ie people and corporations) is entitled to peaceful enjoyment of his or its possessions; no one is to be deprived of them except in the public interest and subject to conditions provided for by law and the general principles of international law.
2. This does not deprive states of the right to enforce such laws as they deem necessary to control the use of property in accordance with the general interest, or to secure payment of taxes or other contributions or penalties.
3. Legal and natural persons may be entitled to human property rights, eg limited liability companies and corporations, so a company's 'human rights' were breached when there was undue delay in reaching a decision following a public inquiry into a plan to quarry on the Scottish island of South Harris (*Re Lafarge Redland Aggregates Ltd* (2000)).

4. A number of different types of human rights violations can be identified although property rights often arise in conjunction with other substantive rights including:

- inequitable treatment of men vis-à-vis women in respect of social security benefits, to which they were disentitled as widowers but would have been entitled were they widows (*Leary v UK* (2000) and *Cornwell v UK* (2000));
- expropriation of assets of a human person (*National & Provincial Building Society etc. v UK* (1997) or legal person (*Air Canada v UK* (1995)).

5. Property rights to which the Protocol refers cover a wide range of subject matter, the European Commission and Court having identified:

- shares (*Bramelid and Malstrom v Sweden* (1982));
- goodwill (*Van Marle v Netherlands* (1986));
- fishing rights (*Baner v Sweden* (1989));
- patents (*Smith Kline and French Laboratories Ltd v Netherlands* (1990));
- ownership of debts or claims (*Greek Refineries etc v Greece* (1994));
- licences (*IS v Netherlands* (1995)).

6. Social engineering and the necessity of maintaining a fair balance between political objectives was tested in *James v UK* (1986) where the Duke of Westminster challenged Leasehold Reform Act 1967 provisions forfeiting the reversion of long leases in favour of tenants who would otherwise have had their homes confiscated, the decision being in favour of the legislation.

7. The limitation rules relating to adverse possession of land were unsuccessfully challenged in *Family Housing Association v Donnellan and Others* (2002) which held that:

   a) they were rules of private law and outside the scope of the Convention;
   b) the purpose was to prevent expropriation of private property by the state;
   c) the 12-year limitation period is adequate to allow dispossessed persons to assert ownership rights.

7.2.3 Right to education Protocol 1 Article 2

1. No one should be denied the right to education, and in the exercise of any functions assumed by the state relating to education and teaching, it shall respect the right of parents to ensure such education and teaching is in conformity with their own religious and philosophical aims.

2. However, the UK entered a reservation because certain provisions of UK Education Acts only required educational services to be provided if they were compatible with the provision of efficient instruction and training and the avoidance of unreasonable public expenditure.

3. The government maintained this stance in 1998 and so kept the reservation when passing the Human Rights Act.

4. The Protocol operates to provide a positive, practical and effective right of access to education, despite its negative wording, so delivery must be in an appropriate language with official recognition of the qualifications to be obtained (*Belgian Linguistics Case supra*).

5. The right can be enforced by:
   a) application of punitive provisions to parents who refuse to comply with compulsory schooling requirements (*Family H v UK* (1984));
   b) disregarding the beliefs of persons other than parents where they have custody of the child, eg adoptive parents (*X v UK* (1977)).

6. States must also respect parents' religious and philosophical convictions:
   a) this extends beyond education into areas such as discipline by corporal punishment (*Campbell and Cosans v UK* (1982));
   b) respecting parents' views does not mean they must be followed or observed, as in choosing single or both sex schooling (*W and others v UK* (1984)).

7. The right to access to education is consistent with the right to establish and run private as well as state schools (*Kjeldson, Busk Madsen and Pederson v Denmark* (1976)), although

state regulation of private schools in order to maintain standards by preventing them from teaching without adequate qualified staff is acceptable (*Jordebo v Sweden* (1987)).

8. The distinction between teaching and indoctrination is not always easy to make, but all schools whether state or private can teach subject matter which includes material that conflicts with the strict religious or philosophical beliefs of parents, provided this is done objectively; opposition to school sex education can be overruled in those circumstances (*Kjeldson etc v Denmark supra*).

7.3 PROCEDURE

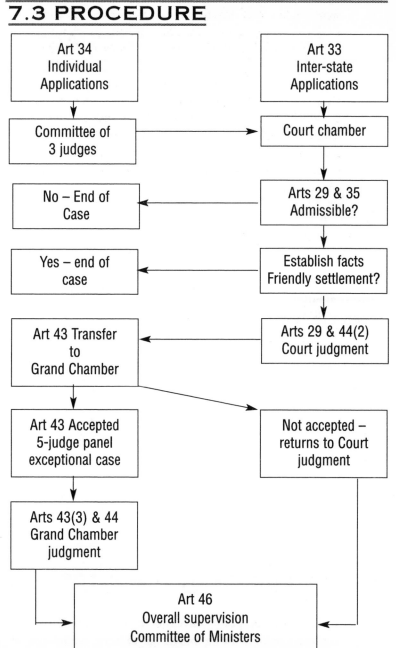

Adapted from D Gomien, D Harris, L Zwaak, Law and practice of the European Convention
on Human Rights and the European Social Charter, *(1996) Council of Europe*

CHAPTER 8

THE HUMAN RIGHTS ACT

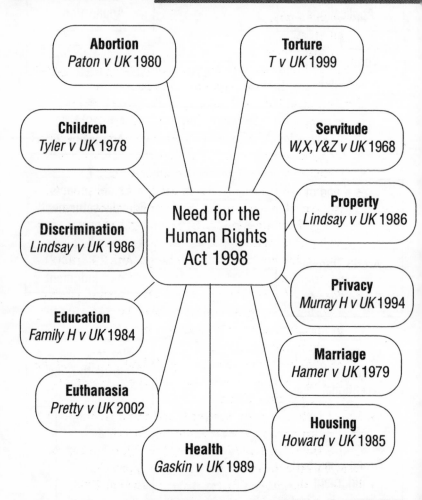

Abortion
Paton v UK 1980

Torture
T v UK 1999

Children
Tyler v UK 1978

Servitude
W,X,Y&Z v UK 1968

Discrimination
Lindsay v UK 1986

Need for the
Human Rights
Act 1998

Property
Lindsay v UK 1986

Privacy
Murray H v UK 1994

Education
Family H v UK 1984

Marriage
Hamer v UK 1979

Euthanasia
Pretty v UK 2002

Housing
Howard v UK 1985

Health
Gaskin v UK 1989

8.1 THE EUROPEAN YEARS 1950–98

1. In 1950 the European Convention established the first
   regional system allowing individuals to bring actions against

states, coming into force in 1953, but the UK did not incorporate the Convention into domestic law, believing there already existed adequate domestic rights and remedies, such as:

- *habeas corpus;*
- jury trial;
- judicial review.

2. After 1966 individuals were permitted to bring cases against the state, but the British government's poor record demonstrated that more protection was needed, eg in:

- *Hamer v UK* (1979) and *Draper v UK* (1980) the Commission ruled that it was an interference with article 12 rights and served no legitimate state objectives or interests to prevent prisoners from marrying;
- *Silver v UK* (1983) the whole panoply of UK procedures and remedies – prison board of visitors, ombudsman, Home Secretary and judicial review – failed to remedy a Sikh prisoner's claim that his correspondence had been unlawfully interfered with contrary to article 8 of the Convention;
- *Malone v UK* (1984) the common law failed to protect British citizens against police telephone tapping, leading to the enactment of the Interception of Communications Act 1985.

3. In the mid-1990s the Labour Party pledged reform, and the Court and Commission were replaced from 1 November 1998 by a full-time Court.

4. Before 1998 UK courts accepted there was a presumption that legislation would not intentionally breach the Convention (*Re M and H (Minors)* (1990)), but there was relatively little interest in the European approach.

5. However, the Human Rights Act was passed in 1998, coming into effect in October 2000, to allow time for adjustment and training, and it:

- provided that existing UK domestic law would be interpreted, and future law enacted and interpreted, by

government and courts in accordance with the
Convention;
- enabled citizens directly to enforce Convention rights in
domestic courts.

8.2 BRINGING RIGHTS HOME 1996

1. Various British historical events and documents have rights
connotations, eg:
   - Magna Carta 1215 (rights to jury trial and due process);
   - Bill of Rights 1688 (shifting balance of power from
Crown to Parliament).
2. Britain's philosophical writing tradition included:
   - John Locke (*Two Treatises on Government*);
   - Thomas Paine (*The Rights of Man*);
   - John Stuart Mill (*On Liberty*).
3. Other factors besides lost cases fuelled the need for change, eg:
   - xenophobic legislation such as the:
     a) Aliens Acts of 1905 and 1914
     b) Commonwealth Immigrants Acts of 1962 and 1968;
     c) immigration statutes of 1990s;
   - Registration of Business Names Act 1916;
   - increasing power of the executive at the expense of
legislature and judiciary.
4. A long-standing campaign by various people over several
decades eventually led to a 1996 consultation paper *Bringing
Rights Home* being published, followed by a White Paper
Rights Brought Home: The Human Rights Bill (Cm3782)
which:
   - made the case for change;
   - explained the government's proposals for enforcing
Convention rights;
   - indicated how this would improve compliance;
   - set out the derogations and reservations which the
government considered necessary.

8.3 THE HUMAN RIGHTS ACT 1998

8.3.1 Further effect to the Convention

1. The Human Rights Act gives 'further effect' to the Convention in a number of ways, s2(1) stating that for interpretation of Convention rights, courts and tribunals must take into account:
   - European Court judgments, decisions, declarations or advisory opinions;
   - Commission reports and decisions;
   - decisions of the Committee of Ministers.

2. For interpreting domestic legislation, s3(1) provides that Acts of Parliament and subordinate legislation (statutory instruments, bye-laws etc) must be read so far as possible compatibly with Convention rights, with the qualification that this does not affect the validity, operation or enforcement of pre-existing legislation.

3. The higher courts are empowered to make 'declarations of incompatibility' under s4 where in any proceedings dealing with primary legislation the Court is satisfied that some provision is incompatible with Convention rights.

4. The higher courts are:
   - House of Lords;
   - Judicial Committee of the Privy Council;
   - Courts Martial Appeal Court;
   - Scottish High Court of Justiciary sitting otherwise than as a trial court or the Court of Session;
   - High Court;
   - Court of Appeal.

5. Where any of these courts is considering making a declaration of incompatibility, notice should be given to the Crown so that the relevant minister or nominee can be joined as a party to the proceedings.

6. The law may then be amended, and failure to do so would lead to probable action in the European Court with the government eventually losing, and accompanied by bad publicity en route.

7. Lower courts lack this power and must follow the legislation, nor can they trigger the s10 remedial order provisions providing a fast track procedure to amend defective legislation; lower courts include county and magistrates' courts and other tribunals.

8.3.2 Incompatibility and illegality

Incompatibility

1. An early example of a declaration of incompatibility was *H v Mental Health Review Tribunal N & E London Region* (2001), concerning the burden of proof on patients seeking release in applications to Mental Health Review Tribunals.

2. The government were obliged to take the following steps:
   - a remedial order was made in November 2001;
   - retrospective approval was granted by Parliament in April 2002;
   - patients subjected to similar injustice could claim compensation.

3. Obligation is imposed on public authorities to act in ways that are compatible with Convention rights under s6:
   - public authorities are courts, tribunals and any person certain of whose functions are of a public nature;
   - Parliament and its activities are excluded.

Illegality

1. Where the Court finds the act of a public authority unlawful, s8 authorises:
   a) such relief, remedy, or order as it considers just and appropriate;
   b) power to award damages, with some restrictions.

2. Public authorities include:
   a) those legislatively designated ie courts and tribunals (s6);
   b) others whose functions are obviously public, eg:
      - government departments;
      - local authorities;
      - police and prison services;
   c) hybrids, eg housing associations (*Poplar Housing and Regeneration Community Association v Donoghue* (2001));
   d) Non-hybrid bodies, eg charities (*R (on the application of Heather) v Leonard Cheshire Foundation* (2003);

3. Convention rights to which the Act gives further effect mean:
   - the rights and fundamental freedoms set out in articles 2–12 and 14 of the Convention;
   - articles 1-3 of the First Protocol;
   - articles 1 and 2 of the Sixth Protocol, as read with articles 16–8 of the Convention, subject to any designated reservation or derogation, as enacted by s1 HRA.

8.3.3 Structure of the Human Rights Act Chapter 42

The Act comprises 22 sections and three schedules.

The Human Rights Act 1998

Introduction

s1   The Convention Rights
s2   Interpretation of Convention
     rights

Legislation

s3   Interpretation of legislation
s4   Declaration of incompatibility
s5   Right of Crown to intervene

Public authorities

s6   Acts of public authorities
s7   Proceedings
s8   Judicial remedies
s9   Judicial acts

Remedial action

s10 Power to take remedial action

Other rights and proceedings

s11 Safeguard for existing human
     rights
s12 Freedom of expression
s13 Freedom of thought, conscience
     and religion

Derogations and reservations

s14 Derogation
s15 Reservation
s16 Period for which designated
     derogations have effect
s17 Periodic review of designated
     reservations

**Judges of the European Court of
Human Rights**

s18 Appointment to European Court
     of Human Rights

Parliamentary procedure

s19 Statements of compatibility

Supplemental

s20 Orders etc under this Act
s21 Interpretation
s22 Short title, commencement,
     application and content

Schedules

Schedule 1 The articles
Part I The Convention rights and freedoms

Sets out the rights and freedoms contained in Convention articles 2–12, 14, and 16–8, from the right to life to limitations on the use of restrictions on rights (see the previous chapter on the Convention for more detail of the actual articles)

Part II The First Protocol

Articles 1–3 deal with protection of property, the right to education and free elections; part II of the HRA sets out the reservation made in 1952 to the right to education, article 2 being accepted by the UK only so far as it is compatible with the provision of efficient instruction and training, and the avoidance of unreasonable public expenditure

Part III The Sixth Protocol

Article 1 abolishes the death penalty and article 2 allows states to make provision for the death penalty in times of war or imminent threat of war

Schedule 2 Remedial orders

Section 10 of the Act gives power to take remedial action where legislation has been declared under s4 to be incompatible with a Convention right, and this schedule makes further provision on procedure, urgent cases and definitions for such action under s10(7)

Schedule 3 Derogation and reservation

This schedule explains why the UK has derogated (part I) or made reservations (part II) from the Convention, the derogation relating to terrorism measures introduced by the government in 1974 arising from the Northern Ireland disturbances and the adverse European Court's decision of *Brogan and others* in 1988

Schedule 4 Judicial pensions

This obliges the appropriate Minister to ensure that there are pension provisions for any holder of a judicial office who serves as a European Court judge, with statutory instruments providing rules in connection with the HRA

8.4   CURRENT ISSUES

8.4.1 Right to life

1. Causes conflict between:
   - law;
   - morality;
   - ethics;
   - religion;
   - human rights.

2. This inter-connectedness was demonstrated in *Airedale NHS Trust (Respondents) and Bland (Appellant)* (1993), where law lords' speeches concerning teenage football fan Anthony Bland, in a persistent vegetative state (PVS) because of a stadium collapse, called on moral philosophy to help conclude that it is permissible to terminate medical treatment and nourishment when all hope of life is gone.

3. Cases such as *NHS Trust A v M* and *NHS Trust B v H* (2001) confirm that where patients are in a PVS, their right to life is not infringed by withdrawal of treatment.

4. In the case of conjoined twins Jodie and Mary the:
   a) Catholic parents' preferred alternative was inaction so that nature could take its course;
   b) Court of Appeal held that the paramount interests of the child should prevail, even though that meant sacrificing one of the infant lives.

5. In Diane Pretty's case her views were known, unlike the two previous ones, and three Convention articles were considered and rejected by the courts:
   - article 3 (inhuman and degrading treatment);
   - article 8 (right to privacy);
   - article 14 (right not to be discriminated against).

6. State law can be amended to achieve humane results in such instances, eg euthanasia laws in the Netherlands and Switzerland, but this has not been done in the UK.

8.4.2 Right to privacy

Protecting individual rights

1. Privacy questions arise in various circumstances:
   - rights of 'ordinary' citizens;
   - celebrities' hurt pride or economic interests;
   - protection of criminals;
   - protection of reputations.

2. Examples include:
   a) *Douglas v Hello!* (2001), where two actors indirectly obtained recognition of their right to privacy by the Court of Appeal developing the common law of breach of confidence;
   b) two child killers obtained court orders preventing the media from disclosing their whereabouts on release from prison (*Thompson and Venables v News Groups Newspapers* (2001));
   c) Maxine Carr, former girlfriend of murderer Ian Huntley, was granted police protection and a new identity on her release from prison.

3. Footballer Garry Flitcroft tried to prevent publication of allegations of adultery with two women, but an injunction was refused (*A v B (a company)* (2002)).

4. The duty of confidence arises where the person(s) subject to the duty (in these cases the media) know or ought to know that the 'victim' reasonably expects to be protected against disclosure.

5. In Jamie Theakston's case he could not prevent publication of reports of his visiting a brothel, although he did prevent photographs being published, as permission ought reasonably to be given for such publication (*Theakston v Mirror Group Newspapers* (2002)).

6. In another case the Court of Appeal indicated that:
   - the fact of a person's being in public life does not of itself mean that any aspect of it can be published;
   - if the public person chooses to lie (in her case about

drug addiction) the press may be allowed to set the record straight (*Naomi Campbell v Mirror Group Newspapers* (2003)).

ID cards

1. Wider questions of public interest arise, and in November 2003 the Home Secretary announced that the government intended to introduce a national identity cards scheme following a consultation period in the previous year, with various implications:
   - publication of a draft bill in mid-2003 reignited concerns about the purpose, scope and human rights implications;
   - the government's own Information Commissioner told MPs he was increasingly alarmed by the proposals;
   - there are government proposals to introduce biometric identification features into driving licences and passports from 2007.

2. Arguments against the use of ID cards are that:
   - they can be used oppressively by totalitarian governments, always possible even in a democracy;
   - governments might extend the range of uses to which they put the data bases which comprise the brain and memory behind the cards.

3. Biometric identification has unfortunate resonances from Nazi and apartheid predecessors, and suggested drawbacks are that:
   - misuse could restrict, control or remove rights of privacy and freedom of movement;
   - tracing terrorists might be followed by tracing criminals, ranging from murderers, bank robbers and paedophiles through speeding motorists to people who talk on telephones in their cars or drop sweet papers in the street;
   - government has an appalling record for mismanaging and overspending on large computerisation programmes

eg the millennium dome, immigration, passports and the Scottish parliament.

4. Properly managed, bringing together different forms of ID might be more convenient for government and citizens, if distrust of government could be overcome and guarantees provided against misuse.

8.4.3 Fair trial

Requisites of fair trial

1. The right to a fair trial involves a wide panoply of issues only touched upon in the Convention's terms, but which include:
   - pre-trial rights such as prohibition of arbitrary arrest and detention;
   - knowledge of the accusation;
   - rights to professional representation and prompt appearance before a judicial tribunal;
   - detention under humane conditions and a prohibition on being held incommunicado.

2. Hearings require:
   - fairness;
   - publicity;
   - competent representation and impartiality of tribunal;
   - presumption of innocence and adequate time to prepare a defence followed by speedy trial, rights to examine witnesses and obtain the services of a competent interpreter;
   - prohibitions on self-incrimination, retrospective criminal sanctions, and double jeopardy.

3. Post trial rights include the right to:
   - appeal;
   - compensation for miscarriages of justice;
   - absence of delay in rectifying injustices.

Inroads into fair trials

1. Some of these rights have been strained or restricted recently, eg:
   - because of terrorism or combating crime;
   - implementing cheaper procedures;
   - removing some trials from jurors who may not understand complex cases.

2. Under the Criminal Justice Act 2003:
   a) s43 deals with applications by the prosecution for certain fraud cases to be conducted without a jury in serious or complex matters:
      - the judge can make an order where the length and/or complexity of the trial is likely to make it so burdensome to the jury that the interests of justice require this to be done;
      - the Lord Chief Justice or his nominated judge must approve the arrangement;
   b) the principle of double jeopardy is breached, ie the rule that people should not be tried twice for the same offence, and once acquitted that should be an end to the matter;
   c) s75 allows certain cases to be retried, and the following ss76–83 cover applications for retrial with s84 referring to the retrial itself.

3. The original rationale of fairness to the accused is counter-balanced by the argument that modern scientific and forensic investigatory methods mean that there may still be evidence available after an acquittal years ago that today would be sufficient to convict the accused.

4. Human rights considerations include:
   - need for certainty and closure;
   - fallibility and misuse of scientific evidence.

8.4.4 Terrorism

Aspects of terrorism

1. Terrorist threats provide government with cogent reasons to curtail liberty, to be weighed against moral ideas of what is right and fair and the provisions of the Convention and domestic law.

2. Emergency powers have been exercised by English law for centuries, and are used to address contemporary threats, perceived or real:
   - *habeas corpus*, to allow an accused to be brought before the courts, can be suspended, although the last occasion was in Ireland between 1866–9;
   - martial law is an extreme form of military rule, when the army takes over in times of war or grave disturbance, not used in Britain since 1780 but implemented in Ireland from 1916–20;
   - emergency powers were used during both world wars and may still be invoked by government to combat terrorism.

The Terrorism Act 2000

1. The present UK legal definition is contained in s1 of the Terrorism Act 2000 and it:
   - comprises threats or actions involving serious violence to people or property which endangers life and creates serious risks to public health or safety;
   - includes interference or disruption to electronic systems where the objective is to intimidate or coerce governments or people in order to advance political, religious or ideological causes;
   - thus comprises a raft of activities, threats and objectives, wide but not all embracing.

2. Excluded is ordinary political protest designed to change government's behaviour, eg:
   - anti-tax increase campaigns;
   - trade and industrial disputes.
3. Neither of these involves the gratuitous and random violence that frequently accompanies terrorist activities, often characterised by:
   - indifference to human life;
   - hatred of people with different beliefs;
   - religious, cultural or political agendas.
4. Such factors are used by government to justify stringent and sometimes repressive measures which themselves violate normally accepted standards of human rights, eg detention without trial.
5. Objectives of the Terrorism Act 2000 were to:
   - reform terrorism law;
   - establish procedures proscribing illegal organisations;
   - make provisions dealing with fundraising;
   - tackle money laundering;
   - improve investigatory procedures.

Anti-terrorism, Crime and Security Act 2001

1. The 2000 Act came into force in February 2001 but the attack on the twin towers in New York on 11 September 2001 led to the Anti-terrorism, Crime and Security Act 2001, with 129 sections, 14 parts and 8 schedules.
2. Provisions covered by the 2001 Act include:
   - forfeiture of terrorist cash and the Treasury's ability to freeze assets, ss1 and 4;
   - denial of refugee status to certain groups of people, ss33 and 34;
   - introduction of criminal liability for making, possessing or exploding nuclear weapons, s47.
3. Persons suspected by the Home Secretary of being terrorists but who cannot be returned to a country where they might be tortured or killed can be detained indefinitely:

- appeal is to the Special Immigration Appeals Commission;
- the suspect and his lawyer are not entitled to see evidence and can be excluded from the hearing if the material is deemed to be secret;
- this is an article 15 derogation from the article 5 right not to be arbitrarily detained, justified by perception that there is a threat of war or sufficiently severe public emergency;
- the House of Lords ruled on 16th December 2004 that the indefinite detention without trial of foreign nationals under emergency terror laws is incompatible with European human rights laws.

4. Part 3 of the Act allows the police to:
   a) seek private and personal information, without warrant or disclosing the fact, by going through government and public department files;
   b) claim that it might be useful to an investigation, whether or not they are likely to find evidence of criminal activities.

5. Under s89 the powers already available in the Police and Criminal Evidence Act 1984 and Terrorism Act 2000 are extended to allow more fingerprinting and retention of records that formerly would have been destroyed.

6. Under part 12:
- the previous practice of using telephone data for billing and then destroying it is removed;
- records must be retained in case they might prove useful in the investigation of future offences;
- confidentiality is thus removed from telephonic communications.

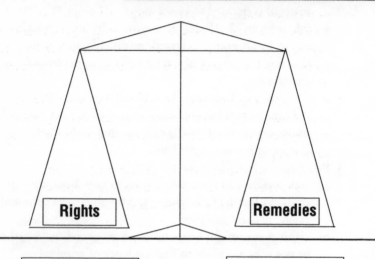

Rights

- collective
- individual
- positive
- negative
- universal
- relative
- enforceable
- aspirational
- fundamental
- theoretical
- achievable

Remedies

- individual
- collective
- courts
- commissions
- UN
- regional
- NGOs
- accountability
- intervention
- humanitarian
- developmental

9.1 SKINNING THE CAT

Ubi jus, ibi remedium: where there is a right, there is a remedy.

9.1.1 Negatives

1. There is more than one way to skin a cat, and a common characteristic of different states is that they develop a variety of remedies and enforcement systems; article 8 of the Universal Declaration provides that everyone has the right to an effective remedy by competent national tribunals for acts violating their fundamental rights as granted by constitution or law.

2. A remedy is available when an authoritative body – court, legislature or other effective agency – enforces compliance with prescribed norms and/or imposes sanctions for failure so to comply.

3. However, international law is problematical, because:
   - customary international law is scant and tenuous compared with the common law;
   - international 'legislation' only governs states so far as they choose to be bound by it, ie by entering into and ratifying treaties;
   - enforcement via the International Court of Justice (ICJ) can only take place when the parties specifically agree to be bound by its jurisdiction; there is no obligatory enforcement mechanism;
   - so, if international law is often unclear, unaccepted, and unenforceable, how far is it 'law' and where is the 'legal system'?

4. Some international legal regimes are enforced more energetically than rights, eg the World Trade Organisation (WTO), so where there is a will there is a way, trade being seen as closer to states' self-interest than human rights, which sit uncomfortably alongside the international law and trade regime because they are:
   - weakly enforceable and enforced;
   - largely aspirational;
   - not the primary focus of most state policy.

9.1.2 Accentuate the positive

1. Nevertheless, many rights are more than aspirational, because:
   - there is some recognition of limited customary effect of the UN Declaration on Human Rights, and the international covenants are widely acknowledged if not always observed;
   - regional regimes have investigatory and/or enforcement machinery;
   - States may have enforceable domestic provisions, eg the Human Rights Act 1998 in the UK.
2. Other enforcement methods are available, eg:
   a) specific sanctions through the UN, particularly:
      - embargo;
      - exclusion;
      - suspension;
      - military force;
      - expulsion;
   b) accountability, ie holding individuals responsible via the ad hoc international criminal tribunal system and the International Criminal Court (ICC);
   c) tackling immunity and removing impunity;
   d) use of truth commissions;
   e) intervention;
   f) positive discrimination;
   g) ombudsmen.
3. These differing tools can:
   - alter preconceptions;
   - counteract human rights abuses;
   - sometimes provide and enforce remedies.

9.2 UN ENFORCEMENT

9.2.1 The Charter

1. Westphalian influence pervades the UN Charter, eg:
   - article 2(4) requires members to refrain from threatening or using force against other states in their international relations;
   - article 2(7) says that nothing in the Charter authorises UN intervention in state domestic jurisdiction, or requires them to submit such matters for UN settlement.

2. Even so, the Security Council sometimes takes action when agreement can be achieved, eg the 1999 Security Council Resolution 1244 authorising implementation of the Kosovo peace settlement, enabling the civil presence (*inter alia*) to:
   - perform basic civilian administrative functions;
   - maintain civil law and order and establish local police forces;
   - protect and promote human rights;
   - assure safe and unimpeded return of refugees and displaced persons.

3. UN action is often too little and too late, eg Rwanda and Bosnia in the early 1990s and the Darfur massacres of the Sudan in 2003–4.

4. UN Charter human rights violation powers may be called 'sanctions' although the Charter does not refer to them as such, but other actions available to the UN include:
   - military force, the most extreme step although rarely used, eg the first Gulf war;
   - the General Assembly, as advised by the Security Council, may suspend states under article 5 of the UN Charter, which means loss of membership privileges to the offending member;
   - exclusion under article 19 of the Charter where a state is in arrears with contributions, although this is not a human rights sanction;

- embargo under article 41 interferes with an offending
  state's economic activities, and although frequently
  hitting the wrong targets, they can:
  a) be used in peace or war time;
  b) restrict imports or exports of goods;
  c) be used as a non-violent method of dealing with a
     recalcitrant state;
  d) deny communications, visitors, and even diplomatic
     relations.

5. Sanctions may be slow but eventually effective, eg as in
   South Africa, and as a final resort offending states may be
   expelled, or withdraw voluntarily to forestall expulsion.

9.2.2 The International Covenants

1. Implementation of the ICESC is dealt with in article 2,
   which contains undertakings from each state party to take
   steps, individually and through international assistance and
   cooperation, particularly economic and technical, to realise
   the rights of the Covenant, including requisite state
   legislation and guarantees of non-discrimination.

2. The ICCPR requires all states to report to the Human
   Rights Commission every five years, and thence to the
   General Assembly via the Economic and Social Committee:
   - indicating which of their domestic laws protect civil and
     political rights;
   - describing domestic provisions that enhance or inhibit
     individuals' rights;

3. The Civil and Political Covenant can be implemented in
   other ways:
   - a state may make an optional article 41 declaration that
     another state is abusing civil and political rights, leading
     to examination by the Human Rights Commission
     (rarely used);
   - under Resolution 1503 of the Economic and Social
     Committee individuals and NGOs can complain of
     human rights violations by states, but these are simply

filed unless a considerable number is received, in which
case the UN has limited power to investigate.

4. Under the optional protocol article 9 of the Covenant,
implementation is strengthened, ie:

- the Human Rights Commission receives and considers
  communications from individuals claiming to be victims
  of violations by member states, once all available
  domestic remedies have been exhausted;
- anonymous communications and those abusive of
  submission rights are inadmissible.

5. Complaints and reporting are not as effective as direct legal
enforcement, and often the complaints mechanism is not
incorporated in a treaty or covenant but must be agreed by
individual states under a Protocol, eg in CEDAW.

6. UN reports are often made by special rapporteurs appointed
to investigate particular or generic human rights problems,
and sometimes NGOs can bring influence to bear.

7. The UN Code of Conduct for Law Enforcement Officials
1979 requires law enforcement officials to:

- fulfil their legal duties while respecting and protecting
  human dignity and maintaining and upholding the
  human rights of all persons;
- use force proportionately and only when strictly
  necessary;
- maintain confidentiality and never use torture or other
  cruel, inhuman or degrading treatment nor invoke
  superior orders as an excuse for misbehaviour;
- protect the health of persons in their custody, combat all
  corruption, and always respect the Code.

9.3 ACCOUNTABILITY

1. The desire for accountability caused the allies to establish
the Nuremberg and Tokyo tribunals after the Second World
War, based on assertions that activities (horrendous though
they were) not previously contrary to international law
would now be criminal, introducing genocide and crimes

against humanity.

2. Although understandable, the tribunals contravened two major rights tenets:
   - they were retrospective;
   - for the Tokyo tribunal, they represented 'victors' justice'.

3. They established a new kind of legal procedure that eventually led via the former Yugoslavia and Rwanda tribunals to the ICC.

4. There is ongoing need for accountability as psychopathic Heads of State and their acolytes continue to be accused of gross crimes, eg:
   - the late President of Uganda, Idi Amin;
   - General Pinochet of Chile;
   - General Noriega of Panama;
   - Jean-Bedel Bokassa, former President of the Central African Republic;
   - the late Pol Pot and the Khmer Rouge.

5. Accountability has connections with:
   - impunity;
   - truth commissions;
   - intervention.

9.4 IMPUNITY

1. Impunity means exemption or immunity from punishment, recrimination or other unpleasant consequences, and to act with impunity is to behave in a way that takes no heed or consideration for the consequences of one's actions.

2. It is the arch enemy of human rights, causing offence to victims, survivors, relatives and all right-thinking citizens, and examples include:
   - avoidance by heads or former heads of state of responsibility for actions undertaken by the state, as in the above examples;
   - efforts by states themselves to provide their citizens with blanket protection, eg:

a) US demands for total immunity against accusations of war crimes;

b) similar demands to exclude all US citizens from the jurisdiction of the ICC.

3. Impunity can be tackled by:

- international cooperative efforts to extradite and try alleged criminals;
- Truth Commissions, used successfully in South Africa to bring some closure that no ongoing set of investigations and trials would have been likely to achieve, and also used in over 20 other states;
- States declining to agree to blanket immunity, eg the Netherlands, Sweden and Germany refusal to sign immunity agreements with the United States;
- Continuing the work of the ad hoc tribunals and supporting the ICC.

9.5 INTERVENTION

1. Intervention is forcible and coercive interference in the internal affairs of a state by one or more other states against the wishes of the intervened state, including lesser actions (such as sanctions or suspension) if they actually have coercive effect.

2. The UN General Assembly has condemned armed intervention and all other forms of interference or attempted threats against the personality of the state or against its political, economic and cultural elements, and the UN Declaration on Principles of International Law concerning Friendly Relations and Cooperation among States (1970) says that no state may use or encourage the use of economic, political or any other type of measures to coerce another state to subordinate its sovereign rights or secure advantages of any kind.

3. Regional treaties such as the Charter of the OAS article 16 also condemn armed intervention, which has been the (often-breached) rule since the Treaty of Westphalia 1648, because states prefer an international order that precludes intervention.

4. The recognition of crimes against humanity, genocide and challenges of impunity mean that intervention is now more likely, although article 2(7) of the UN Charter emphasises that nothing therein authorises the UN to intervene in matters that are essentially within the domestic jurisdiction of any state, the purpose being to maintain sovereignty and territorial integrity.

5. This continues the customary international law position, and the principle has been reaffirmed by the UN General Assembly, eg the:
   - Declaration on the Inadmissibility of Intervention (1965);
   - Declaration on Principles of International Law concerning Friendly Relations and Cooperation among States (1970).

6. Nevertheless, intervention can occur in three main ways, ie by:
   - the UN;
   - individual states;
   - coalitions of states.

7. The following will not normally amount to intervention:
   - criticism;
   - diplomatic sanctions;
   - economic sanctions;
   - boycotts (eg of sporting events);
   - provision of humanitarian aid, if done in accordance with International Red Cross principles and in a non-discriminatory manner.

8. What falls within the domestic jurisdiction of states is not a matter of static settled international law, but there is a school of thought which argues that the UN Charter, read as a whole, is sufficient to displace customary law of non-intervention in serious cases, eg:
   - article 1(3) confirms that the purpose of the UN is to promote and encourage respect for human rights and

  fundamental freedoms in the context of achieving international cooperation;
- article 55(c) makes similar self-standing provision;
- article 56 says that all members pledge themselves to take joint and separate action in order to achieve protection of human rights.

9. The Vienna Declaration and Programme of Action 1993 was unanimous in stating that the promotion and protection of all human rights is a legitimate concern of the international community.

9.6 REGIONAL ENFORCEMENT

9.6.1 African Charter

1. Article 30 established the African Commission on Human and Peoples' Rights to promote those rights and ensure their protection in Africa, and Article 45 requires the Commission to protect peoples' rights under the Charter conditions.

2. Article 55 authorises African individuals, groups and NGOs to file complaints with the Commission against states that have ratified, if they believe violation has occurred.

3. Under Article 58, individuals, indigenous peoples and NGOs may submit complaints alleging a series of serious or massive violations by a state party, but domestic remedies must first have been exhausted, unless they are ineffective.

4. Practical limits apply to admissibility, eg they must:
   - not simply be based on media reports;
   - be submitted within a reasonable time;
   - not relate to settled cases, ie it cannot operate as an additional state appeal.

5. Enforceability may be uncertain:
   - decisions are recommendations that states may adopt at their discretion;
   - but the Commission claims its decisions are authoritative interpretations of the Charter and binding on states parties.

6. Following the Commission decision the Assembly of Heads of State and Government decided on further action and decisions remain confidential unless and until this occurs, under Article 59.

7. Final resolution might thus be stifled, although the Commission may influence governments behind the scenes, and summaries of cases are published in annual reports.

8. The 1998 protocol led to the decision to establish a court, whose effectiveness remains to be seen.

9.6.2 The Americas

1. Most states in the Americas accept the compulsory jurisdiction of the Inter-American Court of Human Rights, which has reduced if not eliminated human rights violations as acts of state policy, previously a pervasive problem.

2. The two organs that supervise compliance with human rights norms in the region (encompassing North and South America and the Caribbean) are the:
   - Inter-American Court of Human Rights;
   - Inter-American Commission on Human Rights.

3. The Commission's powers are broad compared with the global and other regional systems, and include:
   - local visits to states accused of rights violations (visits in loco), now of less importance as the main purpose used to be to bring violations to world attention;
   - adjudication of cases on its own account (the case system), of increasing importance as it allows individuals from OAS member States to file a petition alleging rights violations with the Commission;
   - referring cases to the Court for adjudication, relatively few in number, but important because individuals cannot directly petition the Court;
   - appointing rapporteurs;
   - drafting declarations and treaties.

4. Doubts about the effectiveness of the procedures include:
   - criticism of failure to provide due process led to Peru's

withdrawing recognition of the Court (illegally, according to the Court);

● insistence on continuance of the death penalty has led to some states ignoring Court decisions, eg in the Caribbean.

9.6.3 Europe

1. UK law provides various remedies, including:
   ● compensation;
   ● exemplary and punitive damages;
   ● declaratory judgements;
   ● *habeas corpus*;
   ● equitable remedies, especially injunction, specific performance and restitution;
   ● judicial review.
2. The basic duty in article 1 of the European Convention requires High Contracting Parties to secure to everyone within their jurisdiction the rights and freedoms defined in s1 of the Convention, with two main complaint procedures:
   ● inter-state (former article 24, now article 33);
   ● individual (former article 25, now article 34).
3. Achievement of these objectives is left to individual States, ie:
   ● incorporation is not essential;
   ● responsibility remains with the state, so complaints cannot be made against individuals for alleged human rights violations.
4. The right of individual petition is important, as it:
   ● makes individuals effective subjects of international law, in addition to states;
   ● allows for enforcement of rights at domestic and European level.
5. The right to an effective domestic remedy is contained in article 13, based on article 8 of the Universal Declaration, and says that everyone whose Convention rights are violated shall have an effective remedy before a national authority notwithstanding that the violation has been committed by

persons acting in an official capacity, binding the
Convention to the separate state systems.

6. But interpretation of article 13 is problematical and has led
to awkward questions:

- what is an arguable claim?
- what kind of a national authority is required? eg it need
not necessarily be a court;
- must there be a remedy or an aggregate of remedies?

7. Limitation is also imposed by former article 26, now 35
under Protocol 11, which says that the Commission can
only deal with a matter after exhaustion of all domestic
remedies, and subject to a six-month limitation period, in
order to:

- enable states to rectify breaches if they are willing and
able to do so;
- reduce the volume of complaints to the European Court.

8. Much case law deals with how effective remedies must be,
and some of the substantive articles make more detailed and
specific provision concerning effectiveness, eg:

- article 5(4) dealing with deprivation of liberty;
- article 6(1) governing the right to a fair and public
hearing.

9. Certain policies, eg the margin of appreciation, can lead to
difficulties in assessing the effectiveness of human rights in
the context of different domestic systems and standards.

INDEX

Contractions used in the index are those used in the text and/or those used in the list on p.2.

The law at your fingertips...with **Key Facts**

Series Editors: Jacqueline Martin and Chris Turner

Key Facts has been specifically written for students studying Law. It is the essential revision tool for a broad range of law courses from A Level to degree level.

The series is written and edited by an expert team of authors whose experience means they know exactly what is required in a revision aid. They include examiners, barristers and lecturers who have brought their expertise and knowledge to the series to make it user-friendly and accessible.

Key features:
- User-friendly layout and style
- Diagrams, charts and tables to illustrate key points
- Summary charts at basic level, followed by more detailed explanations, to aid revision at every level
- Pocket sized and easily portable
- Written by highly regarded authors and editors

The **Key Facts** series includes:

Consumer Law	0 340 88758 3	144pp	£5.99	**NEW**
Contract Law, 2nd edition	0 340 88949 7	144pp	£5.99	**NEW**
Employment Law, 2nd edition	0 340 88947 0	160pp	£5.99	**NEW**
Human Rights	0 340 88696 X	144pp	£5.99	**NEW**
Tort, 2nd edition	0 340 88948 9	144pp	£5.99	**NEW**
Company Law	0 340 84586 4	128pp	£5.99	
Constitutional & Administrative Law	0 340 81272 9	106pp	£5.99	
Criminal Law, 2nd edition	0 340 88605 6	136pp	£5.99	
Equity & Trusts	0 340 87173 3	138pp	£5.99	
European Law	0 340 84584 8	136pp	£5.99	
Evidence	0 340 85935 0	152pp	£5.99	
Family Law	0 340 81474 8	168pp	£5.99	
Land Law, 2nd edition	0 340 81563 9	112pp	£5.99	
The English Legal System	0 340 80179 4	120pp	£5.99	

Visit www.hoddereducation.co.uk for full details on how to order.

Unlocking the Law

Series Editors: Jacqueline Martin and Chris Turner

Unlocking the Law is a completely new series of textbooks with
a unique approach to undergraduate study of law, designed
specifically so that the subject matter is readable and that
students are not overwhelmed with page after page of
continuous prose.

The text of each title is broken up with features and activities
that have been written to ensure that students are pointed in the
right direction when it comes to understanding the purpose of
different areas within the course. All titles in the series follow the
same format and include the same features so that students can
move easily from one law subject to another.

The series covers all the core subjects required by the Bar
Council and the Law Society for entry onto professional
qualifications and will expand to include titles on option areas.

Unlocking the Law includes the following titles:

**Visit www.unlockingthelaw.co.uk or
www.hoddereducation.co.uk for full details on how to order.**